THE
MODOC

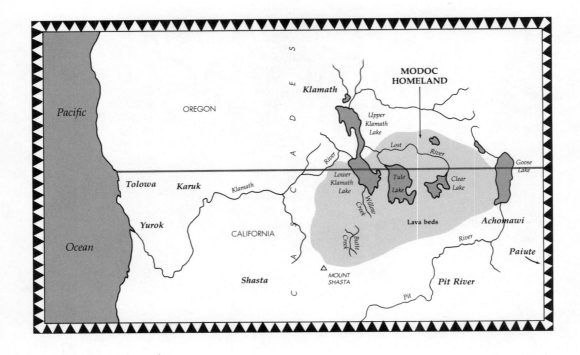

Pacific

Ocean

OREGON

C
A
S
C
A
D
E
S

Klamath

**MODOC
HOMELAND**

Upper
Klamath
Lake

Lost   River

Goose
Lake

River

Lower
Klamath
Lake

Tolowa

Karuk

Klamath

CALIFORNIA

Willnut
Creek

Tule
Lake

Clear
Lake

Yurok

Butte
Creek

Lava beds

Achomawi

Paiute

River

Shasta

△ MOUNT
SHASTA

Pit

Pit River

INDIANS OF NORTH AMERICA

THE
MODOC

Odie B. Faulk and Laura E. Faulk

Frank W. Porter III
General Editor

CHELSEA HOUSE PUBLISHERS
New York   New Haven   Philadelphia

On the cover A Modoc woman's hat made of tule and porcupine quill

Editor-in-Chief Nancy Toff
Executive Editor Remmel T. Nunn
Managing Editor Karyn Gullen Browne
Copy Chief Juliann Barbato
Picture Editor Adrian G. Allen
Art Director Giannella Garrett
Manufacturing Manager Gerald Levine

Staff for THE MODOC
Senior Editor Marjorie P. K. Weiser
Associate Editor Andrea E. Reynolds
Assistant Editor Karen Schimmel
Copy Editor Ellen Scordato
Editorial Assistant Tara P. Deal
Senior Designer Laurie Jewell
Design Assistant Laura Lang
Associate Picture Editor Juliette Dickstein
Picture Research Ilene Cherna Bellovin
Production Coordinator Joseph Romano

Creative Director Harold Steinberg

First printing

1 3 5 7 9 8 6 4 2

Library of Congress Cataloging in Publication Data

Faulk, Odie B.
  The Modoc
  (Indians of North America)
  Bibliography: p.
  Includes index.
  Summary: Examines the history, changing fortunes, and current situation
of the Modoc. Also describes various aspects of their culture.
  1. Modoc Indians. [1. Modoc Indians. 2. Indians of North America] I. Faulk, Laura E. II. Title.
III. Series: Indians of North America (New York, N.Y.)
E99.M7F37 1988   970.004'97   87-24247
ISBN 1-55546-716-4

CONTENTS

INDIANS OF NORTH AMERICA

CHELSEA HOUSE PUBLISHERS

INDIANS OF NORTH AMERICA: CONFLICT AND SURVIVAL

Frank W. Porter III

The Indians survived our open intention of wiping them out, and since the tide turned they have even weathered our good intentions toward them, which can be much more deadly.

John Steinbeck
America and Americans

When Europeans first reached the North American continent, they found hundreds of tribes occupying a vast and rich country. The newcomers quickly recognized the wealth of natural resources. They were not, however, so quick or willing to recognize the spiritual, cultural, and intellectual riches of the people they called Indians.

The Indians of North America examines the problems that develop when people with different cultures come together. For American Indians, the consequences of their interaction with non-Indian people have been both productive and tragic. The Europeans believed they had "discovered" a "New World," but their religious bigotry, cultural bias, and materialistic world view kept them from appreciating and understanding the people who lived in it. All too often they attempted to change the way of life of the indigenous people. The Spanish conquistadores wanted the Indians as a source of labor. The Christian missionaries, many of whom were English, viewed them as potential converts. French traders and trappers used the Indians as a means to obtain pelts. As Francis Parkman, the 19th-century historian, stated, "Spanish civilization crushed the Indian; English civilization scorned and neglected him; French civilization embraced and cherished him."

Nearly 500 years later, many people think of American Indians as curious vestiges of a distant past, waging a futile war to survive in a Space Age society. Even today, our understanding of the history and culture of American Indians is too often derived from unsympathetic, culturally biased, and inaccurate reports. The American Indian, described and portrayed in thousands of movies, television programs, books, articles, and government studies, has either been raised to the status of the "noble savage" or disparaged as the "wild Indian" who resisted the westward expansion of the American frontier.

Where in this popular view are the real Indians, the human beings and communities whose ancestors can be traced back to ice-age hunters? Where are the creative and indomitable people whose sophisticated technologies used the natural resources to ensure their survival, whose military skill might even have prevented European settlement of North America if not for devastating epidemics and the disruption of the ecology? Where are the men and women who are today diligently struggling to assert their legal rights and express once again the value of their heritage?

The various Indian tribes of North America, like people everywhere, have a history that includes population expansion, adaptation to a range of regional environments, trade across wide networks, internal strife, and warfare. This was the reality. Europeans justified their conquests, however, by creating a mythical image of the New World and its native people. In this myth, the New World was a virgin land, waiting for the Europeans. The arrival of Christopher Columbus ended a timeless primitiveness for the original inhabitants.

Also part of this myth was the debate over the origins of the American Indians. Fantastic and diverse answers were proposed by the early explorers, missionaries, and settlers. Some thought that the Indians were descended from the Ten Lost Tribes of Israel, others that they were descended from inhabitants of the lost continent of Atlantis. One writer suggested that the Indians had reached North America in another Noah's ark.

A later myth, perpetrated by many historians, focused on the relentless persecution during the past five centuries until only a scattering of these "primitive" people remained to be herded onto reservations. This view fails to chronicle the overt and covert ways in which the Indians successfully coped with the intruders.

All of these myths presented one-sided interpretations that ignored the complexity of European and American events and policies. All left serious questions unanswered. What were the origins of the American Indians? Where did they come from? How and when did they get to the New World? What was their life—their culture—really like?

In the late 1800s, anthropologists and archaeologists in the Smithsonian Institution's newly created Bureau of American Ethnology in Washington, D. C., began to study scientifically the history and culture of the Indians of North America. They were motivated by an honest belief that the Indians were on the verge of extinction and that along with them would vanish their languages, religious beliefs, technology, myths, and legends. These men and women went out to visit, study, and record data from as many Indian communities as possible before this information was forever lost.

By this time there was a new myth in the national consciousness. American Indians existed as figures in the American past. They had performed a historical mission. They had challenged white settlers who trekked across the continent. Once conquered, however, they were supposed to accept graciously the way of life of their conquerors.

The reality again was different. American Indians resisted both actively and passively. They refused to lose their unique identity, to be assimilated into white society. Many whites viewed the Indians not only as members of a conquered nation but also as "inferior" and "unequal." The rights of the Indians could be expanded, contracted, or modified as the conquerors saw fit. In every generation, white society asked itself what to do with the American Indians. Their answers have resulted in the twists and turns of federal Indian policy.

There were two general approaches. One way was to raise the Indians to a "higher level" by "civilizing" them. Zealous missionaries considered it their Christian duty to elevate the Indian through conversion and scanty education. The other approach was to ignore the Indians until they disappeared under pressure from the ever-expanding white society. The myth of the "vanishing Indian" gave stronger support to the latter option, helping to justify the taking of the Indians' land.

Prior to the end of the 18th century, there was no national policy on Indians simply because the American nation had not yet come into existence. American Indians similarly did not possess a political or social unity with which to confront the various Europeans. They were not homogeneous. Rather, they were loosely formed bands and tribes, speaking nearly 300 languages and thousands of dialects. The collective identity felt by Indians today is a result of their common experiences of defeat and/or mistreatment at the hands of whites.

During the colonial period, the British crown did not have a coordinated policy toward the Indians of North America. Specific tribes (most notably the Iroquois and the Cherokee) became military and political pawns used by both the crown and the individual colonies. The success of the American Revolution brought no immediate change. When the United States acquired new territory from France and Mexico in the early 19th century, the federal government wanted to open this land to settlement by homesteaders. But the Indian tribes that lived on this land had signed treaties with European governments assuring their title to the land. Now the United States assumed legal responsibility for honoring these treaties.

At first, President Thomas Jefferson believed that the Louisiana Purchase contained sufficient land for both the Indians and the white population.

9

Within a generation, though, it became clear that the Indians would not be allowed to remain. In the 1830s the federal government began to coerce the eastern tribes to sign treaties agreeing to relinquish their ancestral land and move west of the Mississippi River. Whenever these negotiations failed, President Andrew Jackson used the military to remove the Indians. The southeastern tribes, promised food and transportation during their removal to the West, were instead forced to walk the "Trail of Tears." More than 4,000 men, women, and children died during this forced march. The "removal policy" was successful in opening the land to homesteaders, but it created enormous hardships for the Indians.

By 1871 most of the tribes in the United States had signed treaties ceding most or all of their ancestral land in exchange for reservations and welfare. The treaty terms were intended to bind both parties for all time. But in the General Allotment Act of 1887, the federal government changed its policy again. Now the goal was to make tribal members into individual landowners and farmers, encouraging their absorption into white society. This policy was advantageous to whites who were eager to acquire Indian land, but it proved disastrous for the Indians. One hundred thirty-eight million acres of reservation land were subdivided into tracts of 160, 80, or as little as 40 acres, and allotted to tribe members on an individual basis. Land owned in this way was said to have "trust status" and could not be sold. But the surplus land—all Indian land not allotted to individuals— was opened (for sale) to white settlers. Ultimately, more than 90 million acres of land were taken from the Indians by legal and illegal means.

The resulting loss of land was a catastrophe for the Indians. It was necessary to make it illegal for Indians to sell their land to non-Indians. The Indian Reorganization Act of 1934 officially ended the allotment period. Tribes that voted to accept the provisions of this act were reorganized, and an effort was made to purchase land within preexisting reservations to restore an adequate land base.

Ten years later, in 1944, federal Indian policy again shifted. Now the federal government wanted to get out of the "Indian business." In 1953 an act of Congress named specific tribes whose trust status was to be ended "at the earliest possible time." This new law enabled the United States to end unilaterally, whether the Indians wished it or not, the special status that protected the land in Indian tribal reservations. In the 1950s federal Indian policy was to transfer federal responsibility and jurisdiction to state governments, encourage the physical relocation of Indian peoples from reservations to urban areas, and hasten the termination, or extinction, of tribes.

Between 1954 and 1962 Congress passed specific laws authorizing the termination of more than 100 tribal groups. The stated purpose of the termination policy was to ensure the full and complete integration of Indians into American society. However, there is a less benign way to interpret this legislation. Even as termination was being discussed in Congress, 133 separate bills were introduced to permit the transfer of trust land ownership from Indians to non-Indians.

With the Johnson administration in the 1960s the federal government began to reject termination. In the 1970s yet another Indian policy emerged. Known as "self-determination," it favored keeping the protective role of the federal government while increasing tribal participation in, and control of, important areas of local government. In 1983 President Reagan, in a policy statement on Indian affairs, restated the unique "government to government" relationship of the United States with the Indians. However, federal programs since then have moved toward transferring Indian affairs to individual states, which have long desired to gain control of Indian land and resources.

As long as American Indians retain power, land, and resources that are coveted by the states and the federal government, there will continue to be a "clash of cultures," and the issues will be contested in the courts, Congress, the White House, and even in the international human rights community. To give all Americans a greater comprehension of the issues and conflicts involving American Indians today is a major goal of this series. These issues are not easily understood, nor can these conflicts be readily resolved. The study of North American Indian history and culture is a necessary and important step toward that comprehension. All Americans must learn the history of the relations between the Indians and the federal government, recognize the unique legal status of the Indians, and understand the heritage and cultures of the Indians of North America.

One-eyed Dixie

THE
EARLY MODOC
WORLD

The world, according to Modoc myth, was a flat disk. Originally it had been quite small. Then *Kumookumts*, the creator, expanded the world, working as if weaving a basket, until the final disk was achieved. Kumookumts named the mountains, rivers, and lakes. Kumookumts, as the creator, was part male and part female but often had the appearance of an old woman.

Kumookumts created the first beings. They lived in this world before the creation of humans. After the first beings had lived a long time, Kumookumts changed them into plants, animals, birds, snakes, insects, and fish— all living things—and gave them their names.

Then Kumookumts created the many tribes of humans by scattering seeds (or perhaps bones) across the earth. One of these tribes was the *Ma Klaks*, which is what the Modoc called themselves. It translates as "people." Another tribe, their close cousins the Klamath, referred to them as *Mo Adok*

Ma Klaks, or "people from the south." To the Modoc, Kumookumts reportedly said, "Though few in number, you will be bravest of all. Even if many and many people come against you, you will kill them." The Klamath were more than twice as numerous as the Modoc. Although they spoke the same language and shared the same culture, the relationship between the Modoc and the Klamath was not always friendly. The Modoc said that when Kumookumts created the Klamath, he said to the Modoc, "You will be easily frightened."

Lastly Kumookumts named the different kinds of food the humans should eat. These were more than 200. As Kumookumts named each type of food, it appeared in the rivers and forests and prairies. Once the food was created, Kumookumts decided who would gather and prepare the food. He said, "Women shall dig roots, get wood and water, and cook. Men shall hunt and fish and fight."

13

After Kumookumts created the human beings and their food, he and the other mythological beings or gods went away. This is why the Modoc refer to Kumookumts in the past tense. In place of himself and the other gods, Kumookumts left spirits through whom humans might influence their world, such as Frog, Rattlesnake, Mole, Fish, Hawk, and Coyote. The spirits could take the form of any animal.

After Kumookumts went away, the spirits held a council that lasted for five years. They made the night and decided that it would be followed by morning. They put the moon in the sky to shine at night and the sun there to light the day. The spirits decided the length of a day and of each of the seasons. Coyote wanted winter to last 12 months, but the others argued that each season should last only 3 months.

One Modoc myth tells of how *Wash*, a female coyote trickster spirit, tried to extend winter to six months. She did this by hanging twice as many moons out as would normally appear during the winter months. Kumookumts learned of this trick and returned to break half the moons, thereby reducing the number of cold winter months to three. He also destroyed Wash by planting sharp tools made of bone in the floor of her lodge so that she was killed when she rolled on them.

Another Modoc legend explains how *Tctuk*, a rock squirrel spirit, was responsible for the snow that falls each winter. Originally snow had been kept in a bag by Kumookumts, but Tctuk allowed snow to escape from the bag, thus creating the cold winters of the Modoc homeland. The Modoc believed that each aspect of the weather, such as wind, snow, thunder, and rain, was a personality with the power to affect the lives of people.

At last the spirits in their five-year council discussed the question, "How long should humans live?" Some of the spirits argued that humans should live forever as did the spirits themselves. Watersnake said, "I want them to shed their skins as I do and become young again." But Mole argued, "I want them to grow old, and get cold when they sit down. Flowers, trees, and everything living must die or the world will get too full." In the end the majority of the spirits decided that humans must get old and die.

Although their world was filled with spirits, the Modoc saw it as a friendly place. The people were optimistic. They saw the land given them by Kumookumts as rich in plant and animal life, and they knew that it would feed and clothe them if they worked hard and prepared themselves for the seasons.

The Modoc of the real world thought that they could reach—and possibly command—the spirits left by Kumookumts through shamans. They believed that a shaman could change the weather, cure the sick, and inflict an illness, or even death, on a victim. Any Modoc—rich or poor, male or female—could become a shaman. A person would receive the call to become a shaman in a dream and then set out alone to find the spirits through whom he or she would work. Any spirit—Frog or Rattlesnake or Fish or Hawk or Coyote—that wanted to work through a particular person would appear during their five-day quest and give that shaman a song. The more songs a shaman had, the greater would be his or her powers. By using the songs appropriately, the shaman could work magic or cures or bring good or bad luck. For these services a shaman was paid, and thus one who was successful could become quite wealthy.

Most Modoc did not pray to the spirit helpers of the shamans. Instead ordinary Modoc prayed to the sun, moon, stars, mountains, rivers, lakes, and to different animals. In their prayers they asked for health, wealth, luck, love, and success in battle. The prayers were generally offered in a sweat house, a tiny, nearly airtight hut. In the hut the Modoc produced steam by pouring water over heated rocks. The steam would heat the air and bring on sweating, which was considered a way to purify the body.

A person could ward off bad luck in various ways. If a watersnake wound itself around a person's leg it meant that the person would have a long life.

From their homeland the Modoc could always see Mount Shasta, snow clad all year round.

A squirrel's tail could bring good luck to men; mole's teeth strung to form bracelets would assure that fortune would smile on women.

The Modoc had many beliefs about animals. For instance, snakes were immortal; each year they shed their skins and became young again. Bears had human intelligence. Doves were forever in mourning because once, when Dove was playing a game and was told his grandmother had died, he had said there would be time to mourn later and continued playing; he has been mourning ever since. The Modoc believed that anyone followed around by a barking coyote or a howling fox would soon die. So would anyone who killed a young bull snake. If an owl was heard hooting near a house at night, it meant someone would soon die. Other indications of an impending death were a dog howling at night in a lonesome manner, a loon making the sound of a neighing horse in the early evening, or stars arranged in a certain way with relation to the moon. Sighting a large shooting star meant that an important person was about to die, and seeing a small falling star meant the death of a child.

The Modoc had no strong concept of an afterlife. However, they did believe that the west was the direction of the "land of the dead." For this reason most Modoc preferred to sleep with their heads facing to the east. The soul might leave the body during sleep, but it would return safely if the head faced away from the west. For the same rea-son the Modoc wanted the doors of their houses to face east. A dead person was cremated with the head facing west. After the body of a loved one was consumed by flames, the living tried to forget the deceased. To dream about a dead person was especially disturbing.

The Modoc were a handsome people of average height, high cheekbones, and dark skin. They hunted and fished, laughed and cried, grew up and had families. They moved about as snows fell and melted, as trees and flowers bloomed in spring, as summer heat ebbed and flowed, as cool autumn winds swept through their lands. They believed that the center of the world was a hill on the eastern shore of Tule Lake.

The Modoc's homeland was a rectangular area of 2,000 to 3,000 square miles near what is now the boundary separating Oregon and California. On the west the Modoc could see the lofty peaks of the eternally snow clad Cascades. To the southwest, rising out of this range was Mount Shasta, a majestic and solitary snow-capped sentinel jutting up from the green forests. To the east of the Modoc's land was a barren area and on the north side were huge forests of ponderosa pine. To the south in the Modoc lands lay lava beds, created about 7,000 years ago when a volcano spewed lava over an area of some 40 square miles. As the lava cooled it contracted and cracked, forming jagged ridges, holes, and crevices. Huge fissures, called crevasses,

The Klamath River, where the Modoc men could catch trout and red suckers.

ran through the area, 10, 20, and even 100 feet deep.

Through their homeland ran the Lost River and numerous creeks and streams. The Klamath River was to the west. Much of their lowland was marshy, while the higher ground was a grassy plain. In this area were four major bodies of water: Lower Klamath, Goose, Clear, and Tule lakes. Non-Indian visitors would later say, as they stood near the lakes and looked up at the surrounding mountains and off into the distance to Mount Shasta, that the region seemed like a little Switzerland.

The waters of this area were filled with such fish as trout, perch, and sucker. The lakes and marshes teemed with ducks, geese, and other water-fowl, especially in winter. Rabbits, squirrels, sage hens, prairie chickens, and other small animals lived on the grassy lands, while in the hills and mountains deer, pronghorn (antelope), elk, mountain sheep, and both brown and grizzly bears roamed. The edible plants included various fruits and nuts, *camas* (lily) bulbs, and *epos* (wild potatoes); *wocas* (water-lily) seeds came from the lakes.

The Modoc's activities followed a standard seasonal pattern over the course of a year. In early spring, when

A winter view of Mount Shasta.

the ice began to break up on the rivers, they left their winter homes. While the men fished for red suckers, the women built drying racks for each day's catch and gathered parsley roots. The fish were dried in the sun and then stored in baskets made of woven dried grass, which the women made as they were needed.

After about a month, the group moved so that the women could begin harvesting epos. To dig for this vegetable they used a small stick that had been held in a fire and hardened at one end. Each woman could harvest about half a bushel of roots a day. While the women dug for epos, the men would make fishnets and catch trout.

By the beginning of summer the men would have started making periodic trips into the mountains to hunt deer, pronghorn, and mountain sheep, while the women began harvesting camas. In between the hunting trips the men continued to fish. In late summer the men would only fish.

At the start of autumn the women gathered berries and fruit, which they dried, and nuts. These were all stored in baskets for winter eating. The men went up into the mountains to hunt deer and elk, after which they returned for another round of trout fishing.

During these months each family prepared its winter store of firewood and food. When snow began to fall and winter gripped the land, a family or group that did not have a good food supply would starve before spring. The Modoc hid their winter food supply in the ground, protected by grass mats and baskets. The location of each family's cache was a jealously guarded secret. If someone stole food the Modoc were not as concerned about punishing the thief as they were about having the food returned. They were an intensely practical people. During the winter the Modoc rested and tried to stay warm; it was a season of little activity.

As the Modoc moved about in small groups during the year, they lived in a variety of homes. Their winter quarters were elaborate and used repeatedly for several years. These were built in villages, of which 21 were located on the shores of Tule Lake, Lost River, Willow Creek, Clear Lake, Goose Lake, and Ness Lake. Three others were located farther away from water.

To erect a winter home, the Modoc builders began by digging a circular pit in the earth. The pit was about 4 feet deep and 16 to 40 feet in diameter. Four major timbers were set upright into the pit to support the roof. Rafters were placed across this framework and covered with mats woven of dried grass. Over this would go a covering of bark or brush, which was then covered with a foot-thick layer of earth removed in digging. A circular hole left at the top served as a vent for smoke and as an entryway. A person entering the home would climb across the roof, into the hole, and down a ladder.

Inside the house there was a fire pit, which provided heat. A bare area was left around the pit, but the rest of the floor was covered with several inches of cut grass. Those living in the house slept on mats made of tule, a type of rush, covered with fur robes. Cooking was done outside in a small house made of grass mats. The Modoc homes lasted three or four years before the timber rotted.

When the Modoc were moving about gathering food, they generally lived in easily constructed earth-covered houses. Sometimes they built smaller versions of their winter homes, roofed only with mats.

During the warmest months of summer the Modoc constructed a third type of house. This type consisted of willow poles set in the ground in a circle, tied together at the top, and covered with mats. It was the smallest of the dwellings.

Two to three families usually shared living quarters because the work of several people was required to build these homes. The women shared the cooking chores, producing two meals a day in winter, three in summer. The men worked together to hunt and fish. The Modoc's land was fertile and productive, but the people had to work steadily to get their year's food supply.

The Modoc clothing was as functional as their homes. For winter wear, moccasins, leggings, hats, shirts, skirts, and robes were made from furry animal hides. In summer many of the

A small basket typical of the type of baskets the Modoc used for storage. It was made primarily of tule, a rush that grew abundantly in the Modoc's homeland.

same articles of clothing, as well as loincloths for the men, were made from the plentiful tule or other grasses that grew in the area. The grasses were dried and then woven together to produce the clothes. The woven articles did not last as long as those made of fur, but they were far more easily and quickly made. Additional warmth was gained in winter by wearing robes woven of fur or grass, which were tied around the neck and waist to hold in body heat. All of the clothing was made by the women.

Both men and women might wear a basket-shaped hat on their heads. Those of the men were usually plain, but the women often wove decorative designs into theirs. The hats were waterproof and gave protection from the elements. In winter the preferred hat was of fur and had flaps to cover the ears.

The families living in a village were generally related. Marriages were of great importance to the whole village. Young people expected that their parents would arrange their marriages. When a boy's mother and father decided on a particular girl for him, they told him of their plans. Then they gathered a large quantity of food, and with other close relatives, but without the boy, went to the girl's home. There they presented the food they had brought. The women from both families used it to prepare a meal, and both families ate together.

If the girl's parents favored the proposal, they returned the visit within a short time. This encouraged the boy's parents to gather a large quantity of gifts such as baskets, furs, skins, robes, beads, bows, arrows, quivers, and canoes. These were taken at dusk by a close male relative of the boy to the home of the girl. The girl's relatives would then evaluate the gifts. If the total worth was sufficiently impressive, the messenger would be given a favorable response when he returned the next morning. If the reply was negative, he took home the gifts.

Once a wedding was arranged, it went forward immediately. The girl's family gathered gifts of equal value to those received to be presented to the family of the groom. The bride was dressed in new and elaborate garments and at noon she and the presents were brought to the groom's home. Her arrival marked the marriage of the couple. The bride remained facing a wall for the next four days, eating little and speaking only in whispers. During this time she took no part in the activities of the house. The groom stayed away from the home during these days, returning only late at night.

After the initial four days, the bride began taking part in regular household activities in the home of the groom. After some time, anywhere from a week to a year depending on how long the groom's family could support the couple, the two moved to the bride's family home. There they would live until after their first child was born. Then they usually moved to the village of the groom's parents, although some couples chose to remain with the bride's family.

During this time, both the man and woman undertook adult work. The men hunted, fished, made canoes, and went on war parties, while the women cared for the young, dug roots and bulbs, and prepared and stored food and clothing.

The chief of each village was known as the *la gi*, which translates as "leader." Always a man, he achieved this position by his ability as an orator, his soundness of judgment, diplo-macy, friendliness, and ability to act in a moment of crisis. Of the different qualities, oratorical ability was considered the most important, for in a tribal gathering the way to get people to follow was by argument and persuasive discussion. The members of a tribe did not vote on a new *la gi*, but rather came to recognize the abilities of a man and accepted him as a new leader. A large village might have several leaders who ruled together in council.

A *la gi* did not go along on war parties. Leadership in battle was given to war chiefs. Any man could become a war chief by attracting followers. If a warrior was successful on raids, many would follow him—and this made him a war chief. If he was unlucky or had poor judgment, no one would follow him and he did not become a war chief.

The purpose of the raids was to obtain slaves and valuable goods such as skins and bows and arrows. Anyone wishing to conduct a raid spoke about his desire and gathered warriors. Modoc war parties were usually small, with no more than 10 or 20 warriors from one or more villages. On rare occasions, however, as many as 100

Modoc men used bows and arrows as weapons for raiding and hunting. This bow was decorated in geometric designs with black, red, and orange paint.

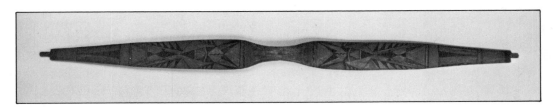

In the summer and autumn the men traveled up into such local mountains as Mount Pitt to hunt deer, mountain sheep, and elk.

might join for a major raid. On such a foray, a war party might include some neighboring Klamath warriors. The raids were usually conducted against the neighboring Pit River Indians, the Paiutes, the Achomawi, or the Shasta. The Modoc despised the Pit River Indians, who were not good fighters. The Paiutes and Achomawi, who shared Goose Lake with the Modoc, were considered inferior. It was from these three groups that the Modoc captured their slaves. The Shasta, however, were feared and respected as excellent warriors who were best left in peace. Once committed to battle, the Modoc were noted as fighters who would not retreat.

When a group of warriors had decided on a raid, they would turn to a shaman to influence its outcome. Any Modoc who wanted to kill an enemy by magic would also turn to a shaman. The Modoc especially turned to a shaman when preparing to gamble.

Gambling at games of chance was a passion among the Modoc. The women played a game in which they used four dice made of beaver teeth. The men's game was far more complicated. One player would arrange his marked playing pieces into a pattern hidden from his opponent. The other player would try to guess the arrangement, making as many preliminary guesses as he wished. The arranger, meanwhile, was free to change the pattern. Each studied the other's face, eyes, and body for clues as to what the other was thinking. At last the guesser would state his final thought as to the pattern and then would be shown what the final pattern was. The players would bet large amounts of goods, and everything a man owned might be gambled away. These games provided great excitement for both men and women. However, because of the risk of starving, the Modoc did not gamble during the winter when they could not easily find more food.

A view from Mount Shasta.

The Modoc followed this life-style for hundreds of years. They were estimated to have numbered between 1,200 and 2,000 before the late 1700s. Then came news of strangers from far away. The newcomers brought horses and guns, along with steel knives, cloth, mirrors, iron cooking pots, and many other goods. When the Modoc saw these things they wanted them, little realizing how their own lives would be changed by acquiring them. ▲

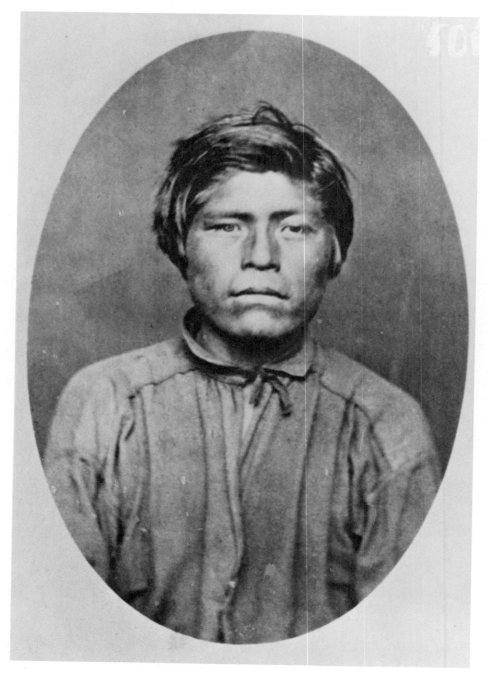

One-eyed Mose

THE
OUTSIDE WORLD
INTRUDES

By the 1790s, American and British merchants were sailing along the west coast of North America, stopping to trade manufactured items for furs with Indians who lived near the shore. The Modoc were too far inland to have any direct contact with these outsiders. However, from neighboring tribes they heard of these strangers, just as they heard of the passage through their region of Meriwether Lewis and William Clark, who were exploring the area in 1805 and 1806, searching for a land route to the Pacific Ocean.

The Modoc's first contact with the outside world was indirect, through the objects brought in by the strangers. Bartering with other tribes that traded directly with the British and Americans, the Modoc began to accumulate steel knives and hatchets, mirrors, cloth, ribbon, glass beads, and iron pots. The outsiders also brought horses and firearms, which would cause a dramatic change in the Modoc's life. When they saw something they thought superior to their own ways, they were quick to adopt it.

By the mid-1830s the Modoc's traditional way of life had already begun to change, but not only from the influence of non-Indians. They were also being influenced by the Plains Indians, whom they met while trading for horses. Following the example of these Indians they abandoned their summer loincloths of tule or grass and winter fur cloaks and now wore clothing made of buckskins. The men also began daubing war paint on their faces when they went on raids.

At first the Modoc avoided direct contact with the whites. They hid whenever they saw non-Indians approaching. Later, in the 1880s, Jeff Riddle, a Modoc, would swear that when the first non-Indians came to Modoc country, his people thought they were evil spirits sent to punish Native Americans.

The first outsiders who actually came through the Modoc's homeland arrived in December 1843. John Charles Frémont came at the head of a surveying and exploring party, and with his companions left the Modoc country

An artist's version of an Indian attack on a wagon train bound for Oregon. All along their route west, settlers encountered resistance from Indians defending their territory.

without incident. In May 1846 Frémont was not as lucky when he returned with a different party. While encamped at Lower Klamath Lake, the group was attacked by Klamath Indians intent on stealing the Americans' horses, and four of Frémont's men were killed. In retaliation the Americans burned a Klamath village. From this point on both the Klamath and Modoc respected the might of the Americans.

During that summer Jesse Applegate and his brother Lindsay led a party of explorers through Modoc country. They were laying out a shorter route for settlers coming from the East to settle in Oregon. By Oc-

tober the Applegate Trail was in use. As the settlers passed through the region, they scared game away from the traditional Modoc hunting area. Lack of food angered the Modoc, and they reacted by attacking wagon trains, killing a reported 24 immigrants in the summer of 1847.

But the Modoc could not attack the diseases brought in by the newcomers. In 1847 an epidemic killed one-third to one-half of the tribe. By 1848 the Modoc nation was estimated to have only 900 surviving members. In retaliation for these deaths, which the Modoc believed were caused by the non-Indians, they attacked several wagon trains bound for Oregon over the next two years. In September 1850 they reportedly killed 80 people on one wagon train alone. The Modoc, mounted on horseback and armed with guns, were gaining a reputation among the intruders as ferocious fighters.

By the end of 1850, however, peace began to return to the Applegate Trail. Few travelers wanted to go to Oregon in 1851. Instead it seemed that the whole world wanted to get to the region south of the Modoc's country.

The change in destination stemmed from the discovery of gold in 1848 in California's American River. The resulting stampede brought hundreds of thousands of people to the area. As more gold seekers arrived, they spread out farther into the region, along rivers and up into the mountains where the gold originated. In March 1851 a prospector named Abraham Thompson found gold on Greenhorn Creek near California's border with Oregon. Almost immediately the towns of Yreka and Shasta Butte City sprang up near the border. The gold miners spread out along the Shasta River. Conflict with the nearby Modoc developed almost immediately.

During the summer of 1851 people from the two new towns moved into Modoc country to gather hay for their horses and mules. As they cut and baled the grass, they scared away the game that the Modoc hunted. The result was incidents of the two sides firing on each other. Later that summer

Jesse Applegate, in a sketch drawn by a relative, George Applegate. After Jesse and his brother Lindsay opened the Applegate Trail through the Modoc's homeland, they settled in the area.

Indians attacked a pack train bound for the goldfield and stole 46 horses and mules. Although the raiders may have been Paiutes or Snakes, the Modoc eventually became owners of the animals, perhaps by trade.

In Yreka about 20 settlers organized into an armed party, determined to recover the animals and punish the Modoc. The group was led by 23-year-old Ben Wright. In a surprise attack at dawn on an unsuspecting Modoc village, Wright and his troops killed several warriors and forced the return of the horses.

The next year skirmishes continued

through the spring and summer. The Modoc killed a few prospectors and repeatedly attacked supply wagons bound for the gold camps. Few gold seekers or settlers paused to think of the hunger they were causing the Modoc by passing through their homeland and driving away the game they hunted for food. Instead they declared that the Modoc had killed more than 20 whites. (Some accounts said as many as 80.) Moreover, stories spread that young women had been captured and were being held by the Modoc.

Ben Wright decided to punish the Indians for these offenses. In November he and his men attacked a Modoc village where the people were drying meat. The surprise was so complete that of the 46 Indian men in the village who tried to defend their families, only 5 escaped. One of them was John Schonchin, who would later become a military leader of the Modoc. Wright and his men scalped the dead Indians and returned to Yreka, where

A wood engraving shows prospectors looking for gold in streams and rocks in California. Magazine and book prints showed easterners what was happening out West.

John Schonchin, a military leader of the Modoc. This painting is based on an 1873 photograph.

they were given a heroes' welcome. California declared Wright and his party to be state militia and paid them for their "service"; Wright received $744 as the leader. After this attack on the Modoc, General John E. Wool, commander of the U.S. Army's Division of the Pacific, wryly commented that he felt it was the Indians who now needed protection, not the whites. And Colonel James B. Fry, one of Wool's officers, said that "the heathen treasured up the example these Christians set him."

Throughout the 1850s there were repeated killings in the Modoc country. Indians and non-Indians alike made unprovoked attacks. When asked about the situation, General Wool remarked, "The future will prove that this war has been forced upon these Indians against their will." With the outbreak of the Civil War in 1861, however, most army troops were pulled out of the area and brought back East to the main theater of operations. This emboldened the Modoc and other Indians in southern Oregon and northern California to intensify their attacks on unprotected settlers.

The winter of 1861–62 was disastrous. The snows were heavy, and the spring had record rains of 70 inches and more. The unusual weather drove away game and killed plants. The Modoc became so hungry that some went to Yreka to seek work. Old Schonchin (father of John), their principal chief, talked openly of asking the U.S. government for the same kind of treaty he had learned other Indians were arranging. The treaty would provide the Modoc with a reservation on which they could live and annuities, yearly distributions of food and supplies. In return the Modoc would give up some of their land.

Among the young warriors who opposed a treaty was *Keintpoos* (or *Kintpuash*). When this young man first went into Yreka, he was jokingly named Captain Jack because he resembled a man who lived there named Jack. In Modoc councils Captain Jack spoke strongly against a treaty with the government, saying he did not want to be confined and made to become a farmer like other Indians on reservations. He wanted no plowing lessons, he said, and other young men agreed with him. By gaining influence

A view of Yreka, California. The town sprang up in the early 1850s after gold was discovered near the California/Oregon border.

and a following, Jack became a war chief among the Modoc, but he was never recognized as a la gi.

By 1863 the U.S. government was able to send some troops back to southern Oregon. Fort Klamath was built that year near the north end of Upper Klamath Lake, north of Lost River. Meanwhile, the farmers and ranchers who continued to move into the region were looking hungrily at the land claimed by the Modoc. They wanted the Indians confined to a small reservation and the remaining acres opened to settlement by non-Indians. In 1863 the Bureau of Indian Affairs in

Washington, D.C., appointed Elisha Steele, a judge in Yreka whom the Modoc had come to trust, Indian agent for the tribes in that area.

Early in 1864 Chief Schonchin decided that the time had come to make a treaty with the government. Ranchers were already moving onto Modoc land, and conflict was sure to follow. Bitterly Schonchin complained that the newcomers were unable to tell the difference between the Modoc and other Indian tribes in the area. The Modoc, he claimed, had been blamed—and attacked—for raids by Shasta, Snake, and Pit River Indians. The fighting had lasted about 20 years, and the Modoc had suffered. Schonchin concluded, "I think if we kill all white men no more will come. We kill and kill but, all time, more come and more come like grass in spring. I throw down my gun."

On February 14, 1864, Chief Schonchin, representing all of the Modoc, approached Elisha Steele to ask for a treaty. However, he did not realize that Steele no longer was the Indian agent for the area. A political foe of Steele had gotten him replaced soon after he had been appointed. Nonetheless, Steele wanted peace between the Indians and settlers so much that without authorization he proceeded to negotiate. They agreed that the Modoc would live in peace and allow non-Indians to pass unmolested through their country. The Modoc would also visit towns only after getting a pass from army officers at Fort Klamath. In return, Steele promised to work to get them their own reservation on the west side of Tule Lake.

Settlers in Oregon were upset when they heard about this agreement because it did not confine the Modoc to a reservation. Nor did it remove them from the Tule Lake area, which the ranchers coveted. Because of these objections—and because the treaty was negotiated by someone who was not an official agent—the Bureau of Indian Affairs decided that a new treaty would have to be drawn up. No one seemed to care that Captain Jack and all the Modoc were keeping an agreement that they had made in good faith. The Modoc believed that Steele had the authority to negotiate. They had made a treaty with him and they were honoring its terms.

J. W. Perit Huntington, superintendent of Indian affairs for California, arrived to negotiate the new treaty. At Fort Klamath in October 1864, Huntington concluded an agreement with the chiefs of the Modoc, Klamath, and Paiute tribes, generally known as the Council Grove Treaty. It called for one reservation in Oregon (just north of the California/Oregon border) for members of all three tribes. Huntington thought these Indians were so much alike they could live together in peace.

In return for giving up all of their lands, the treaty stated that the three tribes would get $8,000 worth of supplies during the first five years the treaty was in force. During the second five years, they were to get another $5,000 worth of supplies, and in the third five years they would get $3,000 in supplies. Schools would be opened, and the Indians would be taught agriculture and mechanics along with reading and writing English. In addition, the treaty called for the government to erect trade shops and mills on the reservation where the Indians could be trained. Confining the Indians and teaching them a trade, Huntington believed, would take them from "their present wild and barbarous mode of life" and "turn their attention to more civilized pursuits."

The major flaw in this treaty, the

Keintpoos, known as Captain Jack, in an 1873 photograph. He was the longtime leader of a dissident band of Modoc who preferred their traditional way of life to living on a reservation.

Modoc and Paiutes agreed, was that it forced them to settle on territory that had been Klamath land. Captain Jack and the young warriors loudly protested this portion of the agreement, but they were forced reluctantly to accept it. Chief Schonchin likewise was unhappy, but he also signed the paper, feeling that he did not have much choice if he wanted to help his people. He promised that he would follow the government's terms exactly. The Modoc moved to the reservation and began to build homes and enclose land for cultivation.

When the Modoc realized that Elisha Steele was no longer their agent, they asked that Lindsay Applegate be named to work with them. They knew and trusted Applegate. Huntington agreed, and Applegate was appointed their agent in September 1865. However, he could do little for the Indians because the government was slow to approve the Council Grove Treaty. Not until 1870, almost six years after the Indians had signed it, was it proclaimed to be in effect. Until then, Applegate had practically no money and could do nothing to build the shops, mills, and schools that had been promised.

Meanwhile, there had been yet another war between the Indians and settlers. Almost immediately after signing the Council Grove Treaty, the Paiutes had fled the Klamath Reservation. Three years of fighting followed. When the so-called Paiute War ended in 1868, the Paiutes reluctantly returned to settle on the north end of the reservation.

During this same period, Captain Jack and his followers left the reservation. They were unhappy that the government had not kept its promises. Moreover, they were constantly being harassed by the Klamath, who stated that the Modoc were living on Klamath land. The Klamath claimed all of the timber, interfered with Modoc fishing, and kidnapped Modoc women for themselves.

In 1865 Captain Jack led his unhappy young warriors south to the Modoc's traditional land along Lost

A main street in Yreka, California. The Modoc traveled to the town to trade in the 1860s.

River. When they arrived, they were surprised to find that non-Indians had already moved into the area. Such settlement was illegal, for the treaty was not yet in effect. The land was still considered to belong to the Modoc.

During the next few years, Captain Jack and his followers hunted and fished along Lost River. They visited in Yreka openly, where they traded horses for goods or bought goods with money they had earned doing odd jobs on ranches or in town. Some even began farming, while others drove teams of horses. During this period Jack's group began wearing the same clothing as their new neighbors, abandoning their buckskins for shirts and trousers of cloth.

Such was the situation in 1869 when Ulysses S. Grant became president of the United States and set out to overhaul the existing Indian policy of the U.S. government. ▲

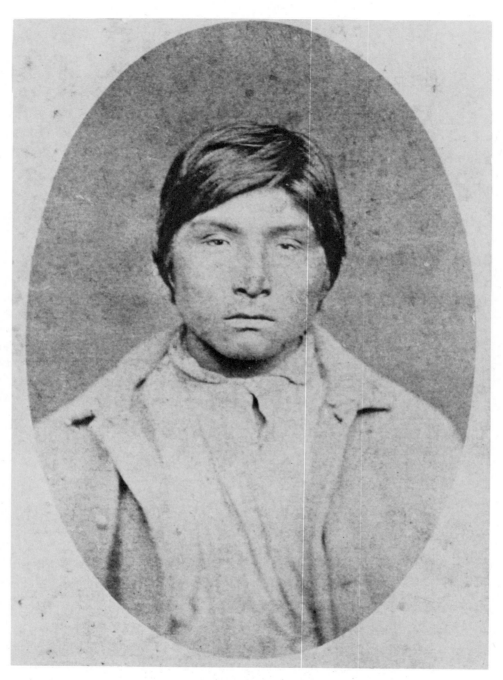

Boston Charley

THE
APPROACH
OF
WAR

With the inauguration of a new president of the United States came new appointments to political office. A new Indian superintendent for Oregon was appointed soon after Ulysses S. Grant took office in March 1869. He was Alfred B. Meacham, a resident of Oregon since 1863 with long experience in Indian affairs. Over Meacham's loud protests, Lindsay Applegate was removed as agent at the Klamath Reservation and replaced by Oliver C. Knapp, a recently retired army captain who quickly proved incompetent.

Meanwhile, Captain Jack and his followers were still living off the reservation. Early in December 1869 Superintendent Meacham called Jack to the agency for a conference. Jack replied that he did not want to see Meacham or Agent Knapp but that if they came to see him, he would talk to them.

The conference was ultimately held on December 22 and 23. At the meeting, Jack accused the whites of being cheats and liars. He denounced the

Council Grove Treaty of 1864 and said that he did not want to return to the Klamath Reservation. One of the shamans, Curley-headed Doctor, was also opposed to returning because on the reservation the power and influence of the shamans were greatly reduced. Jack finally did agree to return, after his sister Mary pleaded with him to do so in order to avoid war and to keep the Modoc tribe united. On December 28 Captain Jack's group and the rest of the Modoc band were reunited on the Klamath Reservation.

Superintendent Meacham did what he could to keep peace among the three tribes on the reservation. He held a council at which he drew boundary lines between the Modoc and the Klamath. He also had Captain Jack and Klamath chief Allen David shake hands, saying to them, "You meet in peace today to bury all the bad past, to make friends.... You are to live as neighbors. This country belongs to you all alike."

The year 1870 began on a hopeful note in southern Oregon, but peace did not last long. Young Klamath warriors could not resist pointing out to the Modoc that they were living on Klamath land. Klamath men stole fence rails and logs cut and sawed by Modoc workers. When Jack complained about this to Agent Knapp, he was promised that things would be "made right." But nothing happened.

When the Klamath found that they would not be punished, they became even more insolent. They took fish caught by the Modoc. They beat the Modoc women gathering wocas seed. And they seized more timber cut by the Modoc. When Jack again protested to Knapp, the agent replied that the Modoc should just move to a place where they would not be bothered by the Klamath.

Captain Jack and his followers moved several miles north, but Klamath tormentors followed, continuing to bully and steal. Yet a third time Jack complained to Knapp. This time the agent responded, "If you come here again, then I will lock you up where the Klamaths will not bother you any longer."

Jack angrily called a meeting of all of the Modoc, despite the absence of Chief Schonchin, who was away fishing. Jack argued that the Modoc should return to their Lost River country and demand their own reservation near Tule Lake. A majority of the tribe voted with him, so Chief Schonchin was forced to agree when he returned.

Agent Knapp stopped issuing rations to the Modoc, stating that they could support themselves through their traditional methods of gathering food. On April 26 Captain Jack, Chief Schonchin, and a majority of the Modoc— 371—left the Klamath Reservation to return to the Lost River area.

Settled back in the vicinity of Tule Lake, the Modoc soon split apart again. Chief Schonchin and 130 followers decided to return to the reservation, while a second group of Modoc moved to Lower Klamath Lake near John A. Fairchild's ranch. This left Jack with some 150 followers, about 60 of whom were warriors.

The ranchers who had moved onto Modoc land near Tule Lake did not welcome Jack and his warriors. But there was peace, despite reports of petty thievery from ranchers in the area and the butchering of some stray cattle. Modoc men traveled to Yreka to visit saloons and stores. In the meantime, Jack tried to collect rent from ranchers. Those who paid the small sums he asked were left alone. Those who refused saw Modoc horses turned loose in their hay fields, and food taken from their homes. When some of the ranchers complained at Fort Klamath, the soldiers laughed. They said that Jack and his few followers wearing cast-off clothing did not seem such a great menace.

Some ranchers and townspeople defended the Modoc, saying they had been cheated out of their land and badly treated by the government. Also

Indian scouts photographed near Tule Lake. Scouts assisted the U.S. Army in locating Captain Jack and his band.

defending the Indians was Brevet Major General Edward R. S. Canby, who assumed command of the U.S. Army's Department of the Columbia, encompassing Oregon and Washington, in 1870. Seeing trouble brewing, Canby warned the War Department that with only 1,225 officers and men to cover the military posts and patrol many thousands of square miles of territory, he had few men to meet any emergency.

Canby also reported that most accounts of Indian raids were exagger-

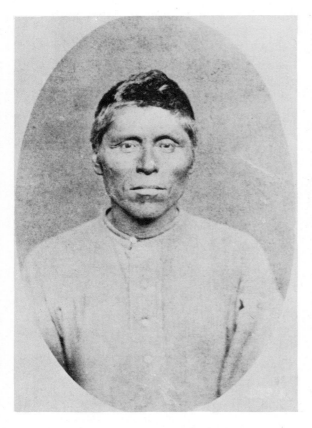

Curley-headed Doctor, a Modoc shaman and warrior, was one of Captain Jack's followers.

ated and that the majority of the raids were committed by Indians who were simply hungry. The rest were the actions of a few individual Indians, not entire villages. During the winter of 1870–71, when settlers complained about Modoc raids, Canby ordered food to be issued to the Indians. This, he felt, would end the problem. In fact it only postponed it.

By 1871 the Council Grove Treaty had been made effective, and what had been Modoc lands around Tule Lake were now being surveyed and opened to settlement. Some new ranchers moved into the area. More would doubtless have moved there had Jack and his followers not been in the vicinity.

In the summer of 1871 some of Jack's followers, such as Curley-headed Doctor, pressed for a war as the only way to obtain their own land and preserve their way of life. However, Jack urged them to be patient. The year before, he had asked Superintendent Meacham for a Modoc reservation around Tule Lake. Meacham had agreed to try to obtain one, and Jack wanted to wait.

Then in June 1871 Jack's niece became ill. Curley-headed Doctor, who usually treated Jack, was away, so Jack sent to the Klamath Reservation for a Modoc shaman who claimed he could cure the girl. When Jack's niece died, Jack promptly killed the shaman. According to Modoc law, Jack was within his rights. Also according to Modoc custom, the dead shaman's kin were correct in wanting revenge. To achieve their goal they cited the treaty of 1864, according to which the Modoc were bound to follow U.S. law. The dead shaman's relatives asked the sheriff of Siskiyou County, California, to arrest Jack as a murderer the next time he came to Yreka. The agency sent Lieutenant Henry Moss from Fort Klamath to take Jack into custody. However, settlers warned Jack about these efforts, and he escaped.

Eventually Elisha Steele advised Superintendent Meacham that the matter should be dropped, saying, "The white people should not meddle with them [the Indians] in their laws among themselves.... Let them settle all these matters among themselves and then our people will be in no danger from them." Meacham, in turn, convinced General Canby of the wisdom of this course of action.

During the summer of 1871 the Modoc were influenced by a new belief that had spread among the Indians. Frank Spencer, a Walker River Paiute Indian, brought the new concept to the Klamath Reservation. The belief had started from a Paiute shaman's vision that the world would be returned to the Indians. The shaman spread the word that there would be great earthquakes that would destroy all humans in the Western Hemisphere. Only a few would be saved. The Indians who would arise from the dead would be those who owned no animals, did not farm, and who had kept the old ways. To hasten this hoped-for change, the faithful ones should paint their faces red with two horizontal black lines on each cheek and perform a special ritual. They should form a circle and hold hands around a fire, chanting and dancing. The dance, where movements were little more than a shuffle, continued for five days. The partici-

pants would stop only at dawn each day to bathe. The Indians called the dance a spirit dance, but among non-Indians it would become known as the ghost dance.

Many Indians were drawn to the ghost dance movement at a time when they had lost hope. The new religion gave them a renewed sense of power. At the Klamath Reservation the agency reported that four ghost dances were held during the summer. Among the Modoc followers of Captain Jack, Curley-headed Doctor stated his belief in the new religious movement and sponsored a dance on Lost River. Despite the hysteria revolving around the new belief, neither the agency nor Superintendent Meacham tried to halt the dancing, although other officials did try to stop similar rituals elsewhere. Several more dances would be held by the Modoc in the months ahead.

Meanwhile, Agent Knapp had resigned at the Klamath Agency, to be replaced by John Meacham, the brother of Alfred Meacham. Superintendent Meacham continued his efforts to get a separate reservation for the Modoc on Lost River near Tule Lake. Despite General Canby's endorsement of the idea, officials in Washington continued to ignore Meacham's request. While the efforts continued, Agent Meacham went ahead and met with Jack. They reached an agreement that allowed the Modoc to stay on Lost River if they promised not to annoy any settlers in the area.

In November 1871 H. C. Tickner opened a new wagon road along Lost River from Yreka to the Modoc country. The road made travel to the region much easier and meant that more homesteaders could come there. The settlers already living in the region realized that their land would rise in value because of the increased demand for it. However, only a trickle of newcomers took advantage of Tickner's road because they feared the Lost River Modoc. To encourage more homesteaders to come, the landowners petitioned Superintendent Meacham to remove the Modoc to the Klamath Reservation and confine them there.

Meacham waited almost two months before acting on this petition, perhaps hoping to receive official approval from Washington of his request for a separate Modoc reservation. Finally in January he notified General Canby of the request, adding that it would take about 50 soldiers to force the Modoc to move to the Klamath Reservation. Meacham ended, "I regret very much the necessity of this action, but the peace and welfare of white settlers and Indians demand that it be done promptly."

At the same time that Meacham was writing to Canby, J. M. True, a settler from the Lost River area, came to Fort Klamath to make the same request on behalf of a group of settlers. Major George G. Huntt, the new commanding officer of the post, forwarded the request to General Canby. Also arriving on General Canby's desk was a petition from 44 settlers of nearby Jackson County, Oregon: "We have been repeatedly on the verge of a desolating Indian war with this band of outlaws who, by your delay to enforce the treaty, have been led to despise rather than respect the authority of the government." They expressed their opinion in the petition that Jack was "a petty Indian chief with twenty desperadoes and a squalid band of three hundred miserable savages."

To the surprise of Superintendent Meacham and all of the settlers, General Canby denied these requests. In his official report he wrote, "I do not think that the immediate application of force, as asked for, would be either expedient or just." Moreover, he said that he did not blame the Modoc for refusing to return to a reservation where they would be exposed to "hostilities and annoyances...from the Klamaths." Canby's immediate superior, Major General J. M. Schofield, commander of the Division of the Pacific, agreed, and no soldiers were sent to dislodge the Modoc from the Lost River area.

Canby, however, did send orders to Major Huntt at Fort Klamath to be ready to protect the citizens of the region, adding that the major was to be prepared to remove Jack and his followers to the Klamath Reservation if such orders arrived from the Bureau of Indian Affairs. Meanwhile, there was to be no war on the Modoc, said Canby, and the bad actions of one or a

General Edward R. S. Canby, U.S. Army commander in charge of the Oregon/ Washington area, defended Captain Jack's band against Oregon settlers.

few individual Indians were not to be an excuse to hold all Modoc guilty.

In the early months of 1872 the Bureau of Indian Affairs finally issued a decision on Superintendent Meacham's recommendations. Bowing to the demands of settlers wanting land, officials in Washington, D.C., decided that there would be no separate Modoc reservation on Lost River. In addition, Superintendent Meacham would be replaced by T. B. Odeneal.

The new appointee had previously been agent to the Osage tribe, located to the east in Indian Territory. He claimed to feel deeply for the Indian tribes: "All my sympathies are enlisted in their [the Indians'] favor when I see any attempt to trample upon their rights." After he had studied the situation at the Klamath Reservation, however, he concluded that Jack and his followers on Lost River were not representative of the Indian people nor of the main body of the Modoc nation. Instead he viewed them as merely outlaws. "I believe," wrote Odeneal, "that to subdue them now is not only the most merciful and Christianlike but the only safe way to deal with them."

Odeneal quickly brought in L. S. Dyar to replace John Meacham at the Klamath Agency. The new agent was not familiar with conditions on the reservation, nor did he understand the struggle between the Modoc and the settlers along Lost River.

In March and April 1872 the agency made efforts to persuade Jack to return peacefully to the Klamath Reservation. During the two conferences that were held, the negotiators realized that Jack was not as firmly in control of his followers as had previously been thought. Jack seemed to want to avoid war, but most of his warriors would not listen to any talk about returning to the Klamath Reservation. For Jack even to talk with the authorities about returning would cost him his position as chief of his band; failure to return to the reservation would bring soldiers and mean war. In one of these talks,

Jack eloquently stated the case of his followers: "We are good people and will not kill or frighten anybody. . . . I do not want to live upon the reservation, for the Indians there are poorly clothed, suffer from hunger, and even have to leave the reservation sometimes to make a living."

Settlers in the area were furious when Jack still remained free and living along Lost River. Army officers noted privately that the true cause of the trouble was land hunger among the whites. Major General Schofield would later write that the Lost River area was "rich grazing land" that was "much coveted by the ranchmen."

In May, Superintendent Odeneal sent members of Chief Schonchin's band on the Klamath Reservation to ask Jack to agree to a third conference. Jack then met with L. S. Dyar, Ivan Applegate, and Oliver Applegate at Juniper Springs near Lost River. The negotiators asked Jack to maintain peace until Superintendent Odeneal and General Canby could decide what to do. To this Jack agreed, but he realized that his request for a permanent reservation on Lost River had been turned down, something the agency had avoided telling him outright.

For Superintendent Odeneal the situation was clear. After reading the report of this meeting, he wrote to the commissioner of Indian affairs in Washington, D.C., requesting troops so that Jack could be arrested. The Modoc, he said, were like children being led by desperadoes. If their leaders were arrested and exiled, the majority of them would accept civilization and "Christian virtues." All would be content to live at the Klamath Reservation under Chief Schonchin if only Jack and his few advisers were out of the way. Among those he wanted to arrest, in addition to Jack, were Curley-headed Doctor and the warriors Scarfaced Charley, Boston Charley, and Black Jim.

In the meantime, to Odeneal's surprise, the cavalry at Fort Klamath was moved some 100 miles north to Camp Warner in the central part of Oregon. When Odeneal protested the loss of military protection, General Canby replied that the commander of the infantry who remained at Fort Klamath had been instructed to keep "a vigilant watch" and "to send an occasional scout through that country." When a July frost wiped out the crops being cultivated at the Klamath Reservation, the Modoc there faced a year of hunger. With the cavalry gone, they could wander freely in search of their traditional food.

July and August 1872 passed quickly. During this time Jack and his followers talked of trying to take up homestead claims of 160 acres each, the same as those available to the settlers, in order to stay along Lost River. They were prospering by gathering food in the old way and were more convinced than ever that they should not return to the reservation,

Captain Jack and his band camped during the fall of 1872 half a mile downstream from this bridge over Lost River.

where they would be dependent on food distributed by the agent. If they could obtain homestead land they would hunt and gather food on this land.

Meanwhile, Superintendent Odeneal was planning to arrest Jack and the other leaders of the renegade Modoc. In July he received permission from the Bureau of Indian Affairs to use military force to make the arrests. The remaining Modoc were to be removed to the Klamath Reservation to live under the leadership of Chief Schonchin.

Odeneal did not move immediately, for he was convinced that the best time to arrest the renegade Modoc leaders was in September when they would be building their winter quarters. In advance of such an effort, General Canby sent the new commander at Fort Klamath, Major John Green, on a scouting trip through the Modoc country along Lost River.

Green left Fort Klamath on September 9, sending scouts in advance to tell Jack that the soldiers were coming to talk, not to fight. Jack refused to meet with Major Green, saying his mother was dying. Green nevertheless proceeded to make a sweep through the area and talked with settlers. He returned to Fort Klamath on October 1. No trouble occurred.

Odeneal seemed in no hurry to arrest anyone—until an order arrived from the Bureau of Indian Affairs in November. He was told to go ahead and arrest Jack and the other Modoc leaders, "peaceably if you can, forcibly if you must." Odeneal informed Canby that he would arrest Jack sometime that month.

Canby, in turn, sent very specific orders to Lieutenant Colonel Frank Wheaton, the district commander in charge of several local posts: "In giving such aid as may be necessary [to Odeneal], you will be governed by your own discretion, the commanding officer suggesting only that . . . the force employed should be so large as to secure the result at once beyond

peradventure [doubt]." Wheaton, in turn, ordered Major Green at Fort Klamath to furnish whatever troops were asked and to inform himself and General Canby if additional troops were needed.

On November 25 Superintendent Odeneal sent Ivan Applegate to Jack's camp to ask the Modoc leader to come to Linkville, a small town that had sprung up along Lost River, for a conference on November 28. With just one companion, Applegate made the trip. He returned to report that Jack refused to come to Linkville, that Jack did not want to talk to Odeneal, and that he would not move to the reservation to live under Chief Schonchin's leadership. Applegate also reported that several of the young warriors, at the urging of Curley-headed Doctor, had pushed Jack to kill him and his companion in order to start a war. Only Jack's vigorous protests had prevented the killing, and the two men had been allowed to leave.

Odeneal was so alarmed—or angry—that he failed to follow the chain of command. Instead of communicating with Colonel Wheaton or General Canby, he sent a messenger to Fort Klamath to demand that Major Green furnish "a sufficient force to compel said Indians to go to . . . said reservation, where I have made provision for their subsistence." Major Green in turn complied without forwarding information about his actions to his district commander, Wheaton, or

Fort Klamath, located at the Klamath Reservation in Oregon, was the U.S. Army's major post in the area of the Modoc homeland.

the commanding general, Canby. He immediately signed an order for Captain James Jackson to take "all available men of his troop" to arrest Jack.

Captain Jackson and 36 men departed Fort Klamath at noon on November 28, 1872, in a cold, freezing rain. Had Major Green waited until more soldiers were present, so that he could confront Jack with a full force, there would probably have been no Modoc War. ▲

Shoknasta Jim

BULLETS
AND
WORDS

Captain Jackson and his troops halted before daylight on November 29. They were about one mile from Jack's village, on the west bank of Lost River. The long ride in a freezing rain had left them numb with cold and quite miserable. Jackson and his second in command, Lieutenant Frazier A. Boutelle, led the 36 soldiers on foot to the Modoc camp. Their orders were to disarm the Modoc and return them, by force if necessary, to the Klamath Reservation.

At the edge of the Indian camp, Jackson halted his soldiers and called out for the Modoc to surrender. He deliberately arrived at dawn to surprise the Indians before they were fully awake and aware of what was going on. A 45-minute conference between the Modoc and Jackson followed, and for a time it appeared there would be no fighting. In fact, some of the Indians, at Jackson's demand, threw down their rifles. Jackson then ordered Lieutenant Boutelle to come forward and take the remaining rifles.

As Boutelle tried to follow this order, he fell into a heated argument with Scarfaced Charley, who did not want to give up his rifle. Scarfaced Charley pointed his rifle at the lieutenant and cocked the hammer. Boutelle responded by drawing his revolver and firing it in return. Then Scarfaced Charley began shooting, while other Modoc warriors picked up the rifles they had thrown down and opened fire. In the five-minute fight that followed, a sergeant was killed and seven soldiers wounded. On the Modoc side, at least one warrior, known as The Watchman, was killed, and several wounded. Several civilians who had gathered to watch the Indians being taken to the reservation were caught in the crossfire, but no one was hurt.

When the shooting started, Jack and his warriors immediately began to move back as they fought off Jackson's troops. The men retreated through the nearby sagebrush, taking a route that would lead them to the lava beds lying to the southwest. After their retreat, the women and children, who had hidden, managed to escape in canoes, following Lost River south into Clear Lake. From there they made their way to the lava beds and joined Jack and the other men. After the shooting ended and the Indians had fled, the soldiers burned what remained of the Indian village.

On the east bank of Lost River, Modoc warriors led by Hooker Jim had been camping. When they heard the shots coming from across the river, they grabbed their guns and moved south around Clear Lake and toward the lava beds. On the way they killed and mutilated the bodies of about a dozen of the civilians who had rushed into the region to take Modoc land. None of the dead, however, were women or children, for the Modoc made war only on men.

The mutilation of the bodies of the civilians killed by Hooker Jim and his men greatly angered the people of Linkville. In the next four days, residents of this village telegraphed demands that the government send sufficient troops to crush the Modoc and force all of them to move to the Klamath Reservation. These demands caused yet a third group of renegade Modoc, led by Shoknasta Jim, to flee to the lava beds.

Shoknasta Jim's band had been living peacefully on land adjoining the ranches of John Fairchild and Pressly Dorris. These two men had lived on good terms with the Modoc for years, giving them a token payment each year for the privilege of grazing their stock on Indian land. When the men of Shoknasta Jim's band heard of the fighting along Lost River, they made it known that they wanted no part of the uprising. Through John Fairchild they sent word to Agent Dyar that they wished to return to the Klamath Reservation.

Before Dyar could send the cavalry to escort them to the agency, however, the people of Linkville organized a lynch party to get revenge for the killings and mutilations committed by Hooker Jim's band. When this group of angry whites arrived at the encampment of Shoknasta Jim and his people, Fairchild and Dorris were there. Anticipating trouble, they had come to persuade the angry mob to return to town. By now, Shoknasta Jim and his people were thoroughly frightened. To avoid going through Linkville on their way to the Klamath Agency, they fled to the lava beds to join Captain Jack and the militants.

Not until December 2, three days later, did General Canby learn of the shootings along Lost River. He did not even hear about them through regular army channels but rather from a sharp note from Oregon's Governor L. F. Grover. The governor had written to ask what the people of his state could do to help the army capture the renegade Indians.

Canby immediately telegraphed Fort Klamath and the reservation to ask what had happened. By December 6 he had reports in hand and was able to inform General John M. Schofield at San Francisco: "There appears to have been a want of proper precaution and preparation for the possible contingency of failure." Canby also reported that he had ordered two companies to move south from Fort Vancouver to Fort Klamath and that a third company would be sent there shortly. Troops soon would take the field to protect the settlers and capture the renegades. Colonel Frank Wheaton would come down from Camp Warner to take personal command of the 225 men in the field. Canby thought that these three companies, along with the troops already in the vicinity, would be able to accomplish the task.

While General Canby was trying to learn the details of what had occurred and get troops to the area, the Modoc were setting up their camp in the lava beds south of Tule Lake. After the vol-

canic lava that created the beds had cooled, deep fissures had formed. Over the years, water had washed out earth and eroded the lava, creating numerous caverns and caves. The largest, known as Ben Wright's Cave, had 15 acres or so of clear space. The cavern held a spring gushing water that was good to drink. Cracks connecting the caves served as tunnels and trenches. Their sides were rough and irregular, allowing the Indians to get good footholds for climbing in and out. The lava beds were a great natural fortification, and the Modoc knew them well. From their hiding places in the lava beds, they could see for miles around and not be visible themselves.

Colonel Wheaton, after viewing the lava beds for himself, wrote to General Canby:

SCENE OF THE MODOC WAR, 1872–1873

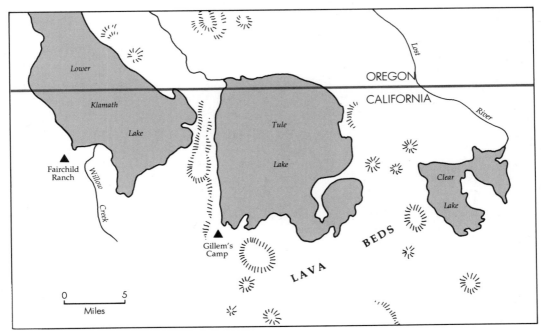

Because of the nationwide interest in the war, photographers posed shots such as this one and sent photographs to the East to be sold.

I have seen something of war and know something of fortifications. I . . . saw many of the great engineering works of the Civil War, but I do not believe that a hundred thousand men in a hundred thousand years could construct such fortifications. A regiment of men could conceal themselves in the caves and fissures and ten thousand men could be marched over them without seeing a man.

Because of rain and the mud, which turned the roads into quagmires, it took the three companies of foot soldiers sent by Canby several days to arrive. Volunteers answering the call of Governor Grover of Oregon were also moving toward the lava beds. Led by Captain John E. Ross, these volunteers arrived ahead of the army because they were mounted and because they came unburdened with supplies. Other volunteers came from California and Oregon. The latter group had been raised by Oliver Applegate from among Indians of other tribes living on reservations.

Also arriving at the scene was Robert D. Bogart, a reporter for the *San Francisco Chronicle*. He immediately wired his paper that both soldiers and civilians were gripped by mass hysteria. In his own words, "Rumor was feeding upon fear and fear feeding upon rumor."

Contributing to the hysteria and rumors were raids by the Modoc warriors who came out of the lava beds. These forays left some volunteers dead and others fleeing in panic. When Captain Jack sent word to the Klamath Agency that he would kill all the Modoc in Chief Schonchin's band who did not come to join him in the lava beds, Oliver Applegate decided to take his volunteers back to Oregon to protect the peaceful Modoc. Meanwhile, Curley-headed Doctor, the shaman, prepared the men for battle by repeating the teachings of the ghost dance.

By the third week in January, 1873, the army had at last gotten its men to the scene of action, and artillery and supplies had arrived. On January 16 Colonel Wheaton wrote optimistically to General Canby, "We leave for Captain Jack's Gibraltar tomorrow morning and a more enthusiastic jolly set of Regulars and Volunteers I never had the pleasure to command."

On the same evening, Curley-headed Doctor was telling the Modoc warriors that his spirits were powerful and would protect the Indians from the harm of white bullets. Captain Jack was not in the mood for battle, however, and was inclined to surrender, as was Scarfaced Charley. But the warriors who had killed civilians did not want to surrender because they believed they would be hanged if they did so. At last, in the Modoc spirit of democracy, a vote was taken. Fourteen warriors voted with Jack to surrender, but 37 sided with Curley-headed Doctor and voted for battle.

The soldiers and volunteers came upon the lava beds at 4:00 A.M. on the freezing morning of January 17. Working their way through the jagged jumble of lava rocks with cold-numbed fingers, they advanced only one mile in more than two hours. Then at 6:30 they opened fire with their cannons and advanced again. As dawn arrived, a thick fog shrouded the area. In ghostlike fashion, Indian warriors appeared in crevasses to shoot, then disappeared before the soldiers could fire in return. Gradually the advance slowed as the soldiers lost their nerve. By evening, 37 soldiers had been killed or wounded. Three volunteers were dead and another nine wounded. Among the Modoc there were apparently no casualties. They came out of their hiding places to take needed weapons and ammunition from the dead on the battlefield and to pick up the supplies discarded by troops retreating in panic.

Colonel Wheaton's report to General Canby was far different from his earlier statements: "In the opinion of any experienced officer . . . , one thousand men would be required to dislodge them from their almost impregnable position, and it must be done deliberately with a free use of mortar batteries." Fighting Indians in the lava beds was far different from battling them in open country.

On learning of the debacle in the field, General Canby relieved Colonel Wheaton of his command, replacing him with Colonel Alvan C. Gillem. A graduate of West Point, Gillem was known to have political influence, which had brought him his promotions. He was widely hated in the U.S. Army because of his unfair dealings with subordinates and he had little experience with Indians.

The last week in January passed without activity. The soldiers waited for their new commander, and a severe snowstorm blanketed northern California. There were extreme shortages of supplies, and the volunteers began deserting in large numbers. Finally by mid-February the storm broke and supplies and men began arriving. At last Colonel Gillem was in place with 700 regulars readied for battle and the supplies to sustain them. But before he could take any action, President Grant was persuaded to try the tactic of negotiation with the Indians.

In Washington, D.C., the former Superintendent Alfred B. Meacham was serving as a member of the electoral college. In January he asked for a meeting with President Grant, during which he persuaded the president to appoint a peace commission to meet with the Modoc. Grant made Meacham the chairman and instructed the commission to learn the cause of the outbreak, find a reservation site that the Modoc would accept, and keep General Canby informed. While the commission was at work, Canby's soldiers were to avoid violence and to protect the local settlers.

The first meeting of the peace commission was on February 18, 1873, at John Fairchild's ranch. Commission members Meacham, Jesse Applegate, and Samuel Case were there and so was General Canby. Applegate and Case demanded that the Modoc be forced to surrender unconditionally, that Indians charged for offenses be turned over to state officials for trial, and that the rest of the renegades be removed to some distant place. Meacham and Canby knew such demands were extreme and made a case for more realistic ones.

The commissioners did agree to send two Modoc women from Chief Schonchin's band to Jack's camp to ask the renegades to meet with them. Jack's reply was conciliatory. "We want no more war and are ready to wash our hands of blood." However, the Modoc did not want Applegate and Case as members of the commission. The two men obligingly resigned, and were replaced by the Reverend Eleazer Thomas of Petaluma, California, and Agent L. S. Dyar of the Klamath Reservation. The newly reconstituted commission met on February 27 and agreed on the terms they would offer to the Indians. The renegade Modoc were to surrender, after which they would be taken to Angel Island in San Francisco Bay. There they would be fed and clothed until a suitable reservation could be found for them. There would be no prosecutions.

Elisha Steele, the Modoc's friend from Yreka, and rancher John Fairchild brought this offer to the lava beds. At first the Modoc seemed inclined to peace, but they kept delaying their reply. Jack would seem disposed to surrender, then turn cold and say he wanted to be left alone. On one occasion he told Steele that he would never return to the Klamath Reservation, adding, "Kill with bullet don't hurt much, starve to death hurt a heap."

Twice Jack promised to surrender, but did not. On March 10 General Canby began moving soldiers into position around the lava beds. Eleven days later he and Colonel Gillem set out to inspect the lava beds personally. To their great surprise they heard shouts coming up from the lava beds from hidden Modoc saying that they wished to talk. When Canby and two officers went forward, they were met by John Schonchin, Scarfaced Charley, and Curley-headed Doctor. A few minutes later Captain Jack came out to join the discussion, saying that all he wanted was to be granted a reservation in the traditional country of the Modoc. Nothing came of this talk because Canby could not make such a promise to the Modoc.

Another meeting was then held, on April 2, with all of the commissioners present. Frank Riddle and his Modoc wife, Toby, served as interpreters. Again Jack presented his demands: a Modoc reservation on Lost River, withdrawal of all soldiers, and no trial of Modoc people in civilian courts. Canby

Frank Riddle (top right) and his Modoc wife Toby (top center), who served as interpreters during and after the Modoc War, pose for photographer Eadweard Muybridge at the lava beds. With them are a military official and four Modoc women who had surrendered.

responded for the commissioners, saying the Modoc must surrender as prisoners of war and the government would dispose of them as it saw fit. No settlement was reached, but the two sides did agree to put up a tent where future talks could be held. It was the rainy season, and neither group wanted to get wet. The tent would be pitched just at the edge of the lava beds, about halfway between the soldiers' line and the location where the Indians had fortified themselves.

Yet another meeting took place on April 5 in the tent. During this talk Jack asked that the lava beds be given to the Modoc people as a home because, as he declared, "nobody will ever want these rocks." The Modoc leader also said that he expected to be killed before any settlement was reached anyway, but he boasted that if he were killed he would not fall on the rocks but rather on top of the bodies of his enemies.

On April 10 the Modoc suggested another meeting for the following day, asking that the commissioners and Colonel Gillem join an equal number of Modoc in the tent. Neither side was to bring arms. Despite Toby and Frank Riddle's warnings to the contrary, Canby thought peace was at hand. That evening he wrote to his wife, "Don't be discouraged or gloomy, darling. I will take good care of myself and come home as soon as possible."

In the Modoc camp the men were quarreling. The militants of the group were determined to force Jack into a fight. They argued that the army had superior numbers and artillery and the Modoc had to do something dramatic in order to win. They wanted to kill the commissioners. But Jack said he wished to end the fighting and return to the reservation. Scarfaced Charley agreed with him. The war party then thrust women's clothing at Jack, saying he was a coward. Jack grew angry and announced that if the majority will was to kill the commissioners, then he reserved the leader's right to kill General Canby. The group decided that Ellen's

Man George would help Jack. John Schonchin and Hooker Jim were to kill Meacham, while Shoknasta Jim and Barncho were to kill Dyar. Boston Charley and Slolux would end the life of Rev. Eleazer Thomas. The evening ended with a ghost dance led by Curley-headed Doctor.

On the morning of April 11 interpreters Frank and Toby Riddle tried to persuade General Canby not to go to this meeting, saying that they feared treachery. Canby laughed, remarking to some of his men, "Well, brother officers, I bid you all a last farewell. From what Riddle says, this is my last day!" Canby's honor as a soldier demanded that he go unarmed, and Thomas put his trust in God and did the same. Dyar and Meacham chose to take derringer pistols.

In the tent they were met by eight Modoc who made little effort to conceal the weapons they were carrying. Canby passed around a box of cigars, and everyone except Rev. Eleazer Thomas began smoking. Jack's first demand was that the soldiers be removed, to which Canby replied that only the president could order this. Jack then proceeded to launch into an angry speech: "If you [are going to] promise me a home, somewhere in this country, promise me today, although I know your promise is not good. This is not much. I am willing to take you at your word." This Canby likewise could not do.

At about 1:00 that afternoon, after the meeting had gone on for a couple of hours, Jack gave the signal, shout-

The April 11, 1873, shooting of General Edward Canby and other officials by the Modoc rebels created a worldwide sensation. This view of the scene, drawn by William G. Simpson and published by the London Daily Illustrated News, *inaccurately shows all of the participants outside. Captain Jack is pointing a pistol at Canby, while the Riddles cower at left.*

ing *"Ot-we kantux-e"* ("All ready"). As he shouted, he pulled out his pistol and fired at Canby. The weapon misfired, whereupon Jack recocked the pistol and shot again. This time the weapon fired properly, and Canby staggered away mortally wounded, a bullet in his head. At the same time Ellen's Man George also shot the general and Boston Charley shot Thomas in the chest. Meacham was struck by a bullet and fell unconscious. Only Dyar managed to escape by running toward the soldiers' camp. Meanwhile, Boston Charley was trying to scalp the bald Meacham. Toby Riddle saved Meacham's life by shouting, "The soldiers

are coming!" At this Boston Charley fled toward the lava beds. Meacham later recovered, although his scalp was disfigured.

The Modoc retreated to their stronghold in the lava beds to wait for the attack they were certain would follow immediately. However, the soldiers did not arrive. Colonel Gillem became overly cautious. Only after several hours' delay did he allow soldiers to advance to the conference tent to learn the fate of Canby and the others.

Reporters who had come to the lava beds and were at the scene were not as cautious. They raced to the

Colonel Alvan C. Gillem's camp at Tule Lake during the Modoc War.

nearest telegraph office to report the death of the only general officer ever killed in an Indian war. Canby's death in a period of peace deeply angered the American public. Newspaper articles, which had previously been favorable to the Modoc, turned hostile. President Grant demanded of his commanding general of the army, General William T. Sherman, that the attack on the Modoc stronghold be so "strong and persistent that their fate may be commensurate with their crime. You will be fully justified in their utter extermination." When he repeated the president's order, Sherman added his own comments: "I hope to hear that they have met the doom they have so richly deserved by their insolence and perfidy."

On April 14 the advance of soldiers under Colonel Gillem began. The cannons kept up their constant pounding, preventing the Modoc from moving about and firing. As the soldiers moved forward, they crossed a rope that Curley-headed Doctor had laid on the ground. He had told the Modoc warriors that any white man who crossed this rope would die. When the soldiers did not die, some of the Modoc began to lose confidence in the shaman. In addition, a Modoc who examined a cannonball died after it exploded. This was also contrary to Curley-headed Doctor's promises that no Modoc could be harmed by white bullets.

On the night of April 16–17 the Modoc asked Jack what they should do. He ordered that the stronghold in the lava beds be abandoned. During the darkness the Modoc used their knowledge of the lava beds to slip past the soldiers. At 11:00 the next morning the troops finally realized that those they pursued were no longer in the lava beds.

Panic spread throughout northern California and southern Oregon. The residents believed the Modoc would ravage the countryside. Troops were sent out in all directions to patrol. On April 26 one company of 64 men on patrol was ambushed by Modoc warriors as it sat down to eat lunch. The 24 who attacked, led by Scarfaced Charley, killed 27 soldiers and wounded 17 others. Getting aid to the survivors of the company was hampered by freezing rain as well as the fear of another Modoc attack. In this skirmish the Modoc lost perhaps one man.

With General Canby's death, the U.S. Army needed to appoint a new commander for the district. They sent Colonel Jefferson C. Davis, a West Point graduate and veteran of both the

U.S. Army soldiers at the lava beds, scene of the Modoc War.

Warm Springs Indian scouts pose near U.S. Army tents. Scouts guided troops in and out of the lava beds during the Modoc War.

Mexican and Civil wars. Quickly he turned the demoralized troops into fighters, as reinforcements of both soldiers and volunteers flooded into the area. Nationwide there was a demand for punishment. One San Francisco newspaper used verse to tell of Captain Jack's taunts to the army:

I'm Captain Jack of the Lava Beds
I'm "Cock o' the walk" and chief of
  the reds.
I kin "lift the ha'r" and scalp the heads
Of the whole United States Army.

One of Colonel Davis's first acts was to end the military career of Colonel Gillem, who had proved a coward on the field. Next he set about building morale among his forces. His efforts were helped by a victory. On May 10 troops defeated the Modoc who attacked south of the lava beds at Sorass Lake. In the fighting Ellen's Man George was killed. This attack was led personally by Jack. Several of the Modoc blamed him for the defeat, and some began to desert. Among those who left were Hooker Jim, Shoknasta Jim, Steamboat Frank, and Bogus Charley. With 10 followers, the 4 fled 40 miles north of the lava beds to hide out on Sheep Mountain.

While army patrols were closing in on Jack and his followers, the renegades at Sheep Mountain decided to surrender. On May 22 they arrived at the army's camp at the lava beds, joined by Curley-headed Doctor. The next day the four war leaders—Hooker Jim, Shoknasta Jim, Steamboat Frank, and Bogus Charley—said they knew where Jack and his people were hiding and that they would persuade them to surrender.

When the leaders met with Jack, he reportedly grew extremely angry. It was these four who had taunted him into killing Canby, and now they wanted him to surrender. He refused to come in. However, his followers were in rags and hungry. By ones and twos they began surrendering to the soldiers, John Schonchin and Scarfaced Charley included. At last on June 1 Jack himself came in to surrender, reportedly saying, "Jack's legs gave out." Colonel Davis immediately ordered a blacksmith to put leg irons on Captain Jack and John Schonchin and then brought them to the army's camp at Clear Lake, where the other prisoners had been taken.

Jack's surrender signaled the end of the Modoc War, a war that had lasted some 190 days. Transporting soldiers to the field, feeding them, and paying their salaries had cost the United States an estimated $420,000. In addition, the government would eventually disburse $74,709.41 to the states of Oregon and California to pay the volunteers who had participated in this campaign. Beyond dollars, the war against Captain Jack and the Modoc had cost a total of more than 400 lives, Indian and non-Indian. The 2,000 acres on Lost River that the Modoc had fought for as a permanent home was valued at the time at only $10,000. ▲

Hooker Jim

A SEARCH
FOR
JUSTICE

Shortly after Captain Jack surrendered, 150 Oregon volunteers commanded by John Ross arrived in the lava bed area. Almost at once they met a dozen Modoc looking for someone to whom they could surrender. Ross accepted them as prisoners, then wired Governor Grover of Oregon, "The Modoc War was ended by the Oregon Volunteers at 12 o'clock last night." Governor Grover responded with his congratulations—and orders for the volunteers to take any Modoc suspected of murdering settlers and turn them over to the sheriff of Jackson County, Oregon, for trial in state courts.

When he heard of these orders, Colonel Davis angrily sent word to Ross that all the Modoc were prisoners of war and not subject to civilian trial. All Modoc suspects were to be tried by a military court, or court-martial, because the crimes they were accused of were committed in a time of war. In fact, Colonel Davis planned to convene

a court-martial, at once. He intended to try those charged with murdering the peace commissioners and any white settlers. On that spot and on that same day he would hang the 7 to 10 warriors he believed would be convicted. This action, he felt, would set an example for any other Indians plotting against the mighty United States.

Davis telegraphed his plan to General Schofield's office in San Francisco and to General Sherman in Washington, D.C. Both generals questioned the legality of Davis's plan to execute the alleged murderers immediately. They ordered him to hold the prisoners and await a study of the proper way to proceed. Sherman's order was clear: Davis was not to hang anyone until the suspects were properly tried and found guilty in a legally convened military court of law. Moreover, those Modoc who had helped locate Jack and had persuaded him to surrender— Hooker Jim, Steamboat Frank, Shoknasta Jim, and Bogus Charley—were

Three participants in the Modoc War—
Shoknasta Jim, Hooker Jim, and Steamboat
Frank—pose with rancher John A. Fairchild
after they were taken prisoner.

to be spared if Davis thought this would encourage other Indians to betray their brothers who rebelled.

Colonel Davis was outraged by Sherman's orders not to proceed with executions. He protested to his superiors, "Delay will destroy the moral effect which their prompt execution would have upon other tribes as also the inspiring effect upon the troops."

Far angrier than Davis were the civilians in the area, as four unarmed Modoc men and their wives and children learned soon after they surren-

dered to John Fairchild at his ranch. As Fairchild was taking them in a wagon to the army camp at Clear Lake, two settlers stopped the wagon, forced Fairchild to get down from the driver's seat, and killed the four Modoc men. The unidentified killers then escaped. Army officers condemned this slaughter of unarmed Modoc but made no attempt to find the perpetrators. Nor were civilian officials eager to find them. Superintendent Odeneal suggested that Agent Dyar investigate, but Dyar responded that he was too busy. Dyar felt that any investigation should be conducted by a stranger to the area who could be unbiased. However, nothing was ever done about these murders.

Colonel Davis decided that, for the safety of his prisoners, he should move them immediately from Clear Lake to Fort Klamath, a distance of about 100 miles. He may have also decided to leave the lava bed area because so many soldiers were trying to desert.

For the trip to Fort Klamath, Davis ordered leg irons for the 44 male captives but not for the 49 women and 62 children. All of the prisoners were put in wagons and closely guarded. The trip took seven days, during which some Modoc looked for an opportunity to escape. Most of the warriors expected to be executed by hanging. In the Modoc tradition, it was important for the soul to escape from the body at death. Because the soul left through the mouth, death by strangulation, which would prevent the soul from leaving the body, was more terrifying to them than any other type of death.

On the first night of the trip, Black Jim and Curley-headed Doctor, who were chained to each other, tried to run into the woods, but their chain caught on a sagebrush and tripped them as soldiers came in hot pursuit. Another prisoner, Curley-headed Jack, somehow managed to get hold of a pistol. When no one was looking, he pulled it out, put it to his head, and shot himself. He was buried beside the road, and the procession went on toward Fort Klamath.

There a stockade had been erected to hold the prisoners until officials in Washington, D.C., found some legal way to hang a few of the men. The Indians' compound was 100 feet long and 50 feet wide, which gave each Indian about 4 by 8 feet of living space. About one-third of the compound was set aside for the Modoc who had surrendered first and then persuaded Jack to come in. It was in this divided compound that most of the Modoc were placed after they completed their seven-day journey. The prisoners considered to be likely candidates for hanging—Jack, John Schonchin, Barncho, Black Jim, Slolux, and Boston Charley—were kept in the guardhouse in heavy shackles. However, Hooker Jim, Bogus Charley, Shoknasta Jim, and Steamboat Frank were put neither in the guardhouse nor in the stockade. As a reward for having helped to get Jack's surrender, they

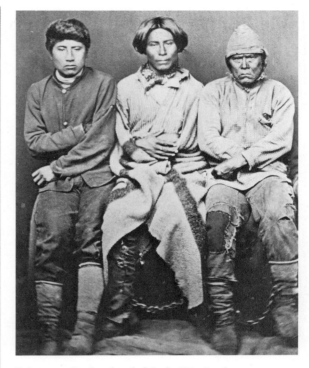

Prisoners Curley-headed Jack, Weuim (or Wheum), known as William Faithful, and Buckskin Doctor. They were accused of killing settlers along Lost River at the start of the Modoc War.

were allowed to move freely around the post.

On June 30, after the Modoc had been in the stockade for about three weeks, U.S. attorney general George H. Williams ruled that only those specifically charged with killing General Canby and the peace commissioners were to be tried by court-martial. All other Modoc had merely committed acts of war and thus should not be tried. The state and county officials of Oregon were outraged by this deci-

Winema, a Modoc Indian known as Toby Riddle, served as an interpreter during the murder trial of six Modoc.

sion, for they wanted the Modoc tried in civilian courts in their state.

Before the court-martial began, Colonel Davis met with Allen David, the Klamath chief, and Old Schonchin, the Modoc chief who had remained on the Klamath Reservation with the majority of the tribe. Also present were Captain Jack and John Schonchin. Toby Riddle acted as interpreter. Davis interrogated the two chiefs, hoping to learn whether the Klamath had

sent arms and ammunition to the rebels, as had been rumored, or if Jack had been encouraged to kill the peace commissioners by the Klamath or the reservation Modoc, as had also been whispered. Both Allen David and Old Schonchin stoutly denied having helped the rebels or having encouraged the murder of anyone. At last Colonel Davis concluded that no proof existed that either the Klamath or the reservation Modoc had aided the rebels.

The court-martial began on July 5. Six officers were assigned to serve as a jury. Lieutenant Colonel Washington Elliott of the First Cavalry was the presiding officer. The officers faced six Modoc: Captain Jack, John Schonchin, Black Jim, Boston Charley, Barncho, and Slolux. Because none of them spoke English with any fluency, they had not understood that they might have hired an attorney to advise them. Without the presence of additional lawyers, the court presumed that they were acting as their own attorneys. So that the proceedings were known to the prisoners as the trial progressed, Frank and Toby Riddle were paid $10 a day to serve as interpreters. The prisoners were allowed to question witnesses, but for the most part they did not fully understand what was taking place.

The officers on this court-martial seemed to understand the drawbacks that the prisoners faced, and they made every effort to allow the six Modoc to tell their side of the issue.

(continued on page 73)

BASKETS, BEADS, AND BUCKSKIN

A woman's necklace made of pine nuts.

Using materials they found in their natural environment, the Modoc created everything they needed in their daily lives. Like other Indians in California, they produced most of these items using local plants and basketry techniques.

Near the lakes and streams in the Modoc homeland grew tule, a type of bulrush, which was the primary material for such items as seed-gathering baskets, eating bowls, mats, loincloths, hats, and gambling trays. The Modoc would keep a supply of dried plant stems and leaves hung up in coils in their homes, ready to be soaked and used whenever needed. The Modoc's technique of basketmaking was plain twining. Two flexible strands (weavers or wefts) were interlaced around stationary vertical elements (the warp).

Modoc baskets were decorated with simple bands of geometric designs. The designs were often twined into the baskets with dark brown tule roots, which could be blackened by immersing the roots in mud. The Modoc also flattened porcupine quills and dyed them with wolf moss, weaving the yellow quills into their baskets. Of all of the Modoc baskets, the women's hats were the most elaborately decorated.

In addition to tule, the Modoc used animal hides and the wood and seeds from trees to craft tools and other items. They made bows and arrows, drums, and necklaces out of these materials. By the mid-19th century buckskin had become the primary material for much of their clothing.

This basket may have been used as a seed container or eating bowl. Shown here enlarged, it is only 4 inches high and 6 inches in diameter.

A woman's hat decorated with interwoven porcupine quills. The Modoc who made this hat named her design "flying geese."

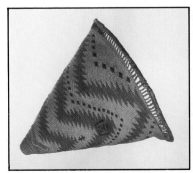

A seed catcher, about 18 inches deep. The Modoc collected seeds by hitting various plants with a racket-shaped beater and catching the falling seeds in baskets.

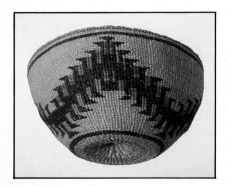

All of these baskets, which were probably used as bowls or short-term containers for food, are about 3 to 4 inches high and 4 to 7 inches in diameter. Like the other baskets included here, they were made around the turn of the century.

A winnowing tray, used to toss wocas and other plants' seeds into the air. The breeze carried off their inedible outer coverings, and the edible, heavier seeds fell into the tray.

A gambling tray, about 18 inches in diameter, on which women played games with dice made of beaver teeth.

A small, finely worked basket made to sell to collectors. The decoration of dark tule roots is more elaborate than that on many Modoc baskets.

Captain Jack's beaded buckskin moccasins from about 1870. The Modoc made jackets and other clothing out of buckskin by the mid-19th century.

A hide dance drum with painted decorations and a drumbeater with feathers. The Modoc's work in hide shows the influence of the Plains Indians.

(continued from page 64)

However, the Modoc understood that they were going to be found guilty and hanged anyway, so they acted either hopeless or defiant and made little effort to defend themselves. Testifying against the defendants were Shoknasta Jim, Hooker Jim, Bogus Charley, and Steamboat Frank. Both Bogus Charley and Hooker Jim admitted to being in the tent when Canby and the peace commissioners were killed, but because they had all been promised immunity by Colonel Davis, they testified willingly. While each witness testified about the murders, the defendants sat in glum silence. Jack later declared, "I cannot talk with chains on my legs." Slolux often slept during the proceedings, and Barncho refused to sit with the others.

The defendants were allowed to speak to the court, and when Jack's turn came, he blamed everyone but himself for all his troubles since childhood. He concluded with a bitter attack on Hooker Jim, who always wanted to fight, as did Bogus Charley, Steamboat Frank, and Shoknasta Jim. These were the people who should be hanged, not himself, said Jack. John Schonchin, in his statement to the court, blamed all the difficulties on the Klamath Indians. The other four said nothing.

After five days, Lieutenant Colonel Elliott announced that the members of the court-martial had found all the prisoners guilty and sentenced them to be hanged on October 3. He also announced that no other Modoc would

Bogus Charley and his wife and child, taken prisoner after the Modoc War.

be tried and that those who had helped track down Jack would be set free, as an example to other Indians that they could "get away with murder" if they helped capture their own people.

Many citizens of Oregon were outraged that only six Modoc were to be hanged. Governor Grover spoke bitterly about the injustice of the situation; meanwhile, ordinary Oregonians demanded blood. On the other side of the continent, in contrast, the outrage

Captain Jack's family after they were taken prisoner. From left, his second wife Lizzy, sister Mary, his daughter, and his first wife.

was exactly the opposite. From Philadelphia, New York, and Baltimore came petitions to President Grant demanding clemency, sent by groups that protested the hanging of any Indians. Especially vocal were the Quakers, known pacifists who had been fighting for Indian rights for almost 100 years. Even Elisha Steele, who was now sheriff of Siskiyou County, California, wrote the president to ask for executive clemency.

John Fairchild added his plea by signing the same letter.

For a time Grant seemed inclined to change the sentences to life imprisonment, but the secretary of the interior and the secretary of war disagreed. At last Grant decided on a compromise: Instead of being hanged, Barncho and Slolux would be sent to Alcatraz for life. However, the two Modoc would not be given this news until they stood at the foot of the gallows.

In the week before the executions, almost 200 people came to Fort Klamath, and a carnival atmosphere prevailed. Reporters came to tell the nation about how the prisoners met their fate.

On the day before his scheduled execution, Jack met with a local minister. To the clergyman he said: "When I look in my heart I see no crime. I was in favor of peace. The young men were not ready for peace—they carried me with them." He felt bitter that the four Modoc who had tracked him down and who had testified against him were to go free. "They have triumphed over me and over the government," he said. When the clergyman spoke of the virtues of heaven and of the beauty of life in the next world, Jack asked the minister if he wanted to go to heaven. When the minister enthusiastically replied that he did, Jack offered him 25 ponies to take his place on the gallows. The minister declined.

At 9:00 A.M. on October 3, as a military band played a quick march, the six Modoc were led out to the scaffold. At this point the sheriff from Jackson County, Oregon, interrupted the proceedings by trying to serve warrants for the arrest of the six men. Lieutenant Colonel Wheaton, commander at the post, turned them down. Next the sheriff served Wheaton with a court order to send the six men to the Jackson County Circuit Court. He refused this order as well. Apparently the people of Oregon did not want the army to hang the six Modoc prisoners. Instead, they preferred to do the job by themselves.

Around the scaffold some 200 soldiers had gathered, along with as many civilians and most of the Modoc and Klamath tribes. In fact, all the Modoc prisoners were ordered to witness the executions. At the foot of the scaffold a blacksmith removed the shackles that had bound the six men. At this point soldiers halted Barncho and Slolux and led them aside. Captain Jack, John Schonchin, Black Jim, and Boston Charley were led up onto the platform. A noose was adjusted around each neck, the four men were seated, and the sentence of the court was read. A chaplain offered a prayer, and the four were hanged. Their bodies were placed in coffins and buried that night.

Later that evening, however, Jack's body was unearthed and taken to the town of Yreka. There it was embalmed, after which it was sent to Washington, D.C. Eventually Jack's skeleton was put on display in a medical museum in the surgeon general's office so visitors could see an example of Indian anatomy.

The executions of the four warriors ended the Modoc War—but not the Modoc people. Their destiny had yet to be determined. ▲

Steamboat Frank

REMOVAL
TO
INDIAN TERRITORY

After the Modoc War, it became apparent that Bureau of Indian Affairs officials had given little thought to what should be done with the Modoc when the shooting stopped. Everyone assumed the renegades would be taken to the Klamath Reservation and forced to stay there under the leadership of Chief Schonchin. No one seemed concerned that keeping the Modoc and Klamath at the same agency had not worked peacefully.

The plan to return them to the Klamath Reservation could not have worked anyway. There were too many angry citizens in the area of the reservation who wanted to punish Jack's followers. Just three days after Jack and his companions were executed, the sheriff of Jackson County, Oregon, once again came before Colonel Wheaton. This time he had warrants for the arrest of other Modoc leaders. The state of Oregon wanted to bring Curley-headed Doctor, Scarfaced Charley, Hooker Jim, and several other Modoc

to trial before a civilian court in nearby Jacksonville for murder and robbery.

As he had done previously, Wheaton refused to honor these warrants on the grounds that, as prisoners of war of the U.S. Army, the Modoc were not subject to state trial. This led to a bitter protest from the governor of Oregon to officials in Washington.

The president and cabinet took up the matter. If the Modoc who had been involved in the war were kept at the Klamath Agency, the government could not guarantee their safety. The state of Oregon would surely arrest some of them when they left the reservation. In addition, local residents would probably do violence to members of the tribe when they had the chance. There was some talk of putting the renegade Modoc on Angel Island in San Francisco Bay, but it would have been too expensive for the government to support the Modoc there, so the idea was dropped. Finally Colonel Davis was ordered to move the renegade Modoc temporarily to Fort D. A. Russell in Wyoming.

On October 12, only nine days after Jack's execution, the forced exodus of his followers began. Leaving Fort Klamath in rented wagons were 39 men, 54 women, and 60 children—153 prisoners of war in all. Waving good-bye to these kinsmen were Chief Schonchin and the approximately 100 Modoc who had stayed at the Klamath Reservation during the war. Escorted by Captain H. C. Hasbrouck and the troops of Battery B, Fourth Artillery, they departed for Redding, California, where they would board a train. At the orders of Colonel Wheaton, the Modoc were not told their destination. Also denied this information were local civilians and reporters.

At Redding, special guards led Barncho and Slolux away in chains. They would be taken to Alcatraz to begin serving their life sentences. The remainder of the prisoners were put aboard an eastbound train. They left in silence. This was the first train ride any of them had ever taken. As the hissing and puffing machine carried the Modoc away from their homeland to an unknown place and future, they felt an overwhelming sense of defeat. None of them would ever again defy agents of the Bureau of Indian Affairs.

When the Modoc and their escorts arrived at Fort D. A. Russell in Wyoming, they were told they would have to continue to Fort McPherson, Nebraska. In Washington further discussions about the Modoc had led to a decision to move them to Indian Territory, an area of land in the middle of the continent set aside by the federal government to resettle many Indian tribes. The superintendent of Indian affairs for Kansas, Enoch Hoag, had wired Commissioner of Indian Affairs Edward P. Smith that "a beautiful

THE OVERLAND ROUTE TO INDIAN TERRITORY, 1873

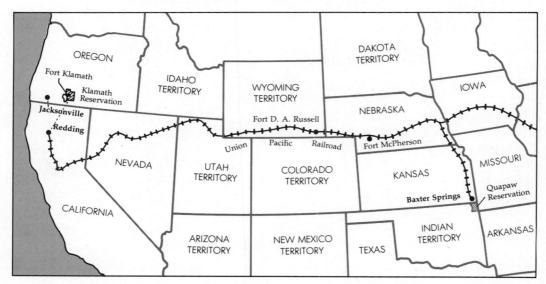

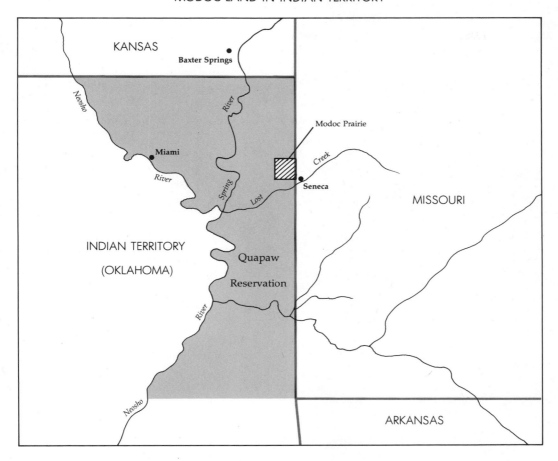

home" for the Modoc could be found somewhere in the extreme northeastern part of Indian Territory. These lands, he said, were "ample, and admirably adapted in climate, soil, delightful rivers and creeks, timber and pasturage for pleasant settlements."

Hoag was referring to land at the Quapaw Agency, a small reservation of about 202,000 acres between the Neosho River and the boundaries of Missouri and Kansas. It was a land of high, rolling prairie and rich soil. On this reservation lived the refugees of other wars: people of the Quapaw, Peoria, Shawnee, Miami, Wyandotte, and Seneca tribes.

The remnants of Captain Jack's band arrived at Fort McPherson on October 29, 1873, and stayed there until mid-November. Then, clad in rags and poorly fed, they were again placed on a train, chained together in cattle cars. This last part of their long journey brought them to Baxter Springs, Kansas, on November 16. Captain

Melville C. Wilkinson, the special commissioner in charge of this leg of their trip, had wagons waiting. In these wagons, still chained, they set out to get a first look at their new home.

During the trip Scarfaced Charley served as the Modoc's chief. The exiled Modoc had not elected him to this position themselves. Instead he had been appointed by Colonel Wheaton while the Modoc were still at Fort Klamath. The colonel had chosen Scarfaced Charley for several reasons. He had not been involved in the murder of the peace commissioners. During the fighting he had protected non-Indians he considered friends. He had fought in the war, but always with honor. In addition, he spoke enough English to have acted as Jack's interpreter during much of the war. Finally, Jack had once said to Colonel Wheaton that he trusted no man, but that if he had to trust anyone it would be Scarfaced Charley.

At Baxter Springs, the women, children, and men unable to work were quartered in the W. Hyland Hotel. In the meantime, the able-bodied men were taken by wagons, not to land set aside for the Modoc but rather to a site just 200 yards from Indian Agent H. S. Jones's house. Jones wanted to keep a close eye on them. Here they were told to build temporary housing for themselves and were given scrap lumber and the services of three carpenters for one day. Within a week the quarters were completed. The buildings, which resembled U.S. Army barracks, were constructed in such a way that the lumber could later be reused. The government spent only $524.40 for the entire project, the total cost including lumber and its freighting and the wages of the carpenters.

During their first winter in Indian Territory, the Modoc suffered terribly. The government had given Agent Jones no funds for their care. Despite regular pleas to his superiors for aid, and despite replies that his requests would get "prompt attention," less than $100 was available for the upkeep of the Modoc. To supplement the small amount of food Jones was able to buy for them, the Modoc men hunted and fished as much as they could. This was still not enough for 93 adults and 60 children. Only gifts from charitable organizations enabled the Modoc to survive. Many people on the East Coast had grown concerned about the plight of the Indians and had formed groups to help them. One organization aiding the Modoc was the Indian Aid Association of Philadelphia, which sent seed for the spring planting and cash that was used to buy shoes and stockings. Among other organizations that helped were the Society of Friends (the Quakers) and the Universal Peace Union.

In the spring of 1874 Jones began negotiating for a permanent home for the Modoc. The final decision was to place the Modoc on 4,000 acres purchased from the Eastern Shawnees for $6,000. This site was most appropriate, reported Agent Jones, for it had more timber, good soil, and water suitable for cultivation and grazing, which he

Members of Alfred B. Meacham's lecture tour of the late 1870s: (left to right) Shoknasta Jim, Steamboat Frank, Frank Riddle, Jeff Riddle, Toby Riddle, and Scarfaced Charley. The Indians were made up and dressed to look like easterners' impressions of what Indians looked like. These costumes were not the Modoc's traditional dress. In his lecture, Meacham advocated the rights of the Modoc and other Indians.

assumed they would need. On June 23, 1874, Jones signed an agreement giving the former Modoc prisoners this land. It came to be known as Modoc Prairie.

During the spring of 1874 one of the first decisions Agent Jones had to reach did not have to do with the Indians' upkeep, but instead with whether some of the Modoc could go on the lecture circuit. The Modoc War had caught the attention of the nation, and several entrepreneurs were trying to cash in on this interest. In May 1873 at Apollo Hall and Wood's Museum in New York City, a melodrama entitled *Captain Jack* had been staged with W. H. Halley playing the Modoc war leader. The *New York Times* reported the work a "sensational drama."

Alfred B. Meacham believed that he could make a profit from his Modoc War experiences by going on a lecture tour in the East. He persuaded Frank and Toby Riddle to accompany him and hoped to attract larger audiences if some Modoc warriors were on stage with him. When Meacham came to the Quapaw Agency to make his request, he found that the Modoc had adapted to their new situation. They were playing croquet. Scarfaced Charley, Steamboat Frank, and Shoknasta Jim were permitted to travel with Meacham over the next three years. His tour never did make him rich, for he discovered that the public was as quick to forget the Modoc War as it had been to get interested in it. To his credit, Meacham included a plea for justice for Native Americans in his lectures.

In 1874 the Modoc children were enrolled in a school at the Quapaw Agency. The school was operated by a branch of the Society of Friends, the Kansas Friends of Indian Affairs. The government provided the building and paid the Friends two dollars per student per week. Attached to the school was a 160-acre farm on which the Quakers kept poultry, horses, and cattle.

At the school the children were taught to read, write, and do sums, and were given a knowledge of geography. There were daily lessons in the Bible, and temperance, abstaining from drinking alcohol, was preached regularly. The girls were given special instruction in cooking, sewing, and housework, while the boys were taught carpentry, animal husbandry, and farming. On the farm the students were taught to raise corn, oats, and

Modoc girls at a day school in the 1890s. Educating Indian children on the reservations was a top priority for the federal government.

wheat as well as vegetables and fruit.

F. H. Smith, representing the Board of Indian Commissioners, visited the Modoc school in September 1874. After his visit he reported great progress. The children were learning English rapidly and several adults were also learning to read and write. He had met with the entire group of Modoc and all of them were happy in their new home. Also, they said they wanted to become like the non-Indians as rapidly as possible.

Before Smith left the reservation he told the Modoc that he would be going on to Oregon. The Indians became visibly excited. They swarmed around asking him to take messages to friends and relatives at the Klamath Reservation, to take photographs of those who had stayed in Oregon, and deliver gifts for them. He was also asked to open discussions about moving to the Indian Territory the 103 Modoc remaining in Oregon.

Smith never did visit the Klamath Reservation, but he contacted Agent Dyar about the prospect of reuniting all the Modoc in the Indian Territory. Dyar studied this possibility and concluded that it might be desirable. The Modoc in Oregon were living on marginal land, not suitable for cultivation, and did not seem inclined to learn non-Indian ways. However, the plan was not kept alive for long. The cost of moving these Modoc to the Indian Territory was estimated at $12,000. Moreover, when agency officials discussed with them the possibility of moving,

the Oregon Modoc were unshakable in their refusal to leave. They wanted to stay where they were. The idea was pursued no further.

On September 13, 1874, Congress at last approved $15,000 for assistance to the Modoc in the Indian Territory. Agent Jones called them together on October 1 and gave each head of a family rations of beef, flour, sugar, coffee, soap, and salt. In addition, new clothing and blankets were issued.

To Jones's great unhappiness, the prospering Modoc at this time renewed their tribal passion—gambling. New blankets became the stakes. Because of his Quaker background, Jones strongly disapproved of the practice. When he demanded that Chief Scarfaced Charley put a stop to it, the chief either would not or could not do so. Agent Jones thereupon replaced him with Bogus Charley. "The change proved acceptable," he noted, "and the moral effect was excellent." Bogus Charley would remain chief until his death in 1880.

By December 1875 Jones reported to the Bureau of Indian Affairs the following: Twenty able-bodied Modoc men had built 12 log houses, each with at least two rooms and a lean-to. They had cut trees and split 17,000 fence rails, which they had used to fence 160 acres. Fifty acres of corn had been planted and harvested, and all of the families had raised sufficient vegetables to see them through the winter. Agent Jones had bought two wagons, two yoke of oxen, and eight cows with calves for the Modoc. By 1877 the Modoc had another 160 acres under cultivation, and Jones had bought them a grain harvesting machine and a revolving hay rake. With the surplus from the allotted Modoc funds, the agent bought them 61 cows and calves that year.

Jones was also pleased to report to his superiors that Bogus Charley had saved enough money to buy a cow and calf. The chief, along with several other Modoc men, had started working on nearby farms in order to get a cash income. Jones had helped them get jobs with their non-Indian neighbors, and he noted that the Modoc worked with greater diligence than anyone thought possible. Modoc men also earned money by hiring themselves out to haul supplies to and from the railroad at Baxter Springs, Kansas. They cut timber from their land, which they sold in Baxter Springs and Seneca, Missouri. And the Modoc women earned money from the beadwork and basketwork that they made and sold to people in the area. In the years following the Modoc used their income to buy themselves buckboards and farm animals, and gradually they prospered.

The Modoc children in the Society of Friends school began to join the Quaker church, as did their parents. Once converted, the Modoc became enthusiastic about their Christianity. A Quaker visitor from Kansas noted in the late 1870s that a fierce blizzard was raging when he arrived. He found a non-Indian meetinghouse empty. But in the Modoc camp, "we saw the Modoc coming from various directions through the storm. There were sixty of them present!" One of the speakers at the Modoc meetinghouse that day was Scarfaced Charley.

Steamboat Frank, too, became a leader in the church. He changed his name to Frank Modoc and became an active speaker not only at the Modoc meetinghouse but also in a nearby non-Indian house of worship. In 1886 he would journey to Maine to get formal training in the ministry, but he died there of pneumonia in 1888 before he could be ordained.

By the late 1870s Agent Jones was delighted to report that the Modoc under his care had increased their livestock herd to 10 horses, 6 mules, 117 cattle, and 227 hogs. They were harvesting more wheat and hay than the much larger Quapaw tribe. Moreover, 50 of the Modoc men and boys were earning money from jobs in nearby towns and on neighboring farms.

The Modoc continued to live peacefully on into the 1880s, taking advantage of educational opportunities, working hard, and making slight economic gains. While Agent Jones was at the Quapaw Agency, he reported the Modoc to be thrifty, peaceable, sober, and hardworking people. He noted that whenever there was a problem, the Modoc tended to listen to the Quaker missionaries at the agency and to follow their instructions.

In 1888 the new agent, J. V. Summers, said that the Modoc were the most advanced of the eight tribes administered by the Quapaw Agency. "The Modoc are good workers," he reported. "The Indians of this tribe dress better, farm more intelligently, add to their improvements, keep their houses cleaner, cook their food better, and send their children to school tidier each succeeding year."

Despite the material progress made by the Modoc in Indian Territory in the 1870s and 1880s, their population was decreasing. When Alfred Meacham had visited the Quapaw Reservation in 1874, he had noted that the tribe had decreased from 153 to 139. Four years later only 103 Modoc were still alive. Then Hooker Jim died in 1879, Bogus Charley in 1880, and Shoknasta Jim in 1881. In 1886 Agent Summers reported a Modoc population of only 91. Three years later there were 86.

Officials in Washington, D.C. had become alarmed at the population decline and had asked Agent Summers to look into the problem in 1885. That year three Modoc were permitted to travel to Oregon to see if there was room for the entire group to return to the Klamath Reservation. In 1886 eight sick Modoc were allowed to move there. According to the Quapaw Agency physician in 1888, the only explanation for this decline could be malaria, which was rampant in the area.

However, other factors were also at work. Adjustment to a harsh climate and a new way of life contributed to the Modoc's decrease in number. Also,

the former renegades were aging. Long Jim, who had been the youngest warrior at the lava beds, died in 1891, and Scarfaced Charley in 1896. Slolux, one of the two Modoc sentenced to Alcatraz had been pardoned after five years in prison and returned to the Indian Territory. There he changed his name to George Denny and lived until 1899.

Curley-headed Doctor, the shaman, also died during this period, in 1890. The Modoc in Indian Territory seemed to have forgotten their ancient tribal religious beliefs soon after making their home on the reservation. Yet many Modoc said that Curley-headed Doctor's death was caused by his spirits, which had grown unhappy with him. According to reliable witnesses, Curley-headed Doctor, as he lay on his deathbed, declared, "As soon as I die, the spirits leaving me will cause the greatest storm you have ever seen." And at the exact moment of his death, Modoc Prairie was struck by one of the worst storms ever. His body was cremated in the traditional Modoc manner, at his wish. His death marked the end of an era for the Modoc. As a shaman and warrior he represented a former way of life, a way of living now gone for the Modoc.

Before the death of Curley-headed Doctor, however, events were taking place in Washington, D.C., that would once again bring change for the Modoc. ▲

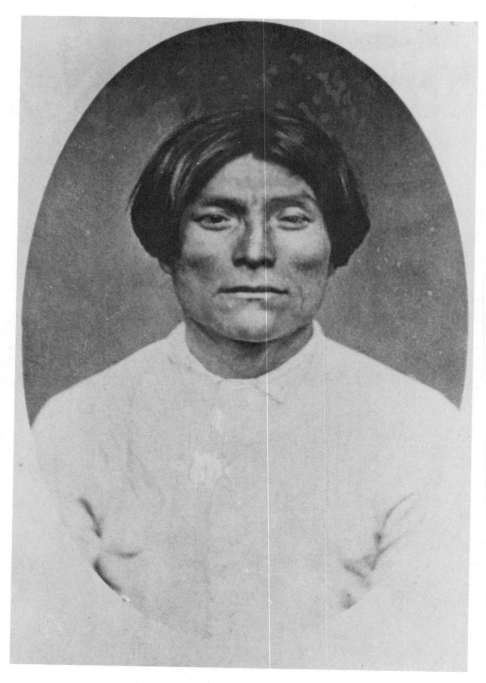

Black Jim

ALLOTMENT, REUNION
AND
MODERN TIMES

In 1887 Congress passed the General Allotment Act, also known as the Dawes Act. It called for an official survey of all Indian reservation lands, after which homesteads of equal size were to be given, or allotted, to individual Indians. The government's intent was to bring to an end the Indians' special status as wards of the government and have them become like other Americans.

On October 10, 1891, Indian Commissioner T. J. Morgan sent 68 land patents to the Quapaw agent on October 10, 1891, made out to individual "members of the Modoc tribe ... for lands in the Indian Territory." Heads of families and other adult men and women would each receive 160 acres.

After they received their land allotments in Indian Territory, some Modoc returned to Oregon to live. In 1899 the census showed 50 Modoc men, women, and children living at the Quapaw Agency. The agent at that time reported that the Modoc, the

most thrifty of all the tribes at his agency, were cultivating all or part of their allotted land and that he did not know "of one able bodied man or woman of this tribe who is not willing to work if he or she received compensation for his or her effort."

However, farming their homesteads in what would soon become the state of Oklahoma proved hard work. Most of the Modoc's acreage had poor drainage and was easily eroded. There were many years with heavy fall rains, which washed out late-season crops. The Modoc who owned livestock made money by selling their surplus animals. Generally the families remaining in Oklahoma survived because they earned some cash income working for non-Indian farmers in the area.

Several of the Modoc who went back to the Klamath Reservation became unhappy and soon decided to return to Oklahoma. The primary reason was that they experienced far greater prejudice in Oregon than they had in

The Klamath Indian baseball team from Yainax, Oregon, in 1905. When some Modoc returned from Indian Territory to the Klamath Reservation in the early 1900s, they found that their former neighbors had changed.

Indian Territory. Because of this prejudice they found few economic opportunities off the reservation. Many who went to Oregon visited their relatives for a time and then decided to return to Oklahoma.

In 1909 Congress recognized the economic and educational progress made by the Modoc in Oklahoma. That year all of the survivors in Oklahoma were ordered reinstated on the rolls of the Klamath Agency in Oregon. This meant they would be eligible to receive allotments and benefits there in addition to those they had received

in Oklahoma. Members of the Klamath tribe were unhappy that the Oklahoma Modoc would be given some of their land, but Congress's instructions prevailed and each Modoc on the tribal roll received 160 acres. At this time yet more Modoc returned to Oregon.

From their new land allotments the Modoc were able to gain extra income. They could use the land themselves, or it could be fenced and leased to ranchers in the vicinity who wanted to cut hay or graze cattle on it.

In addition to Klamath Agency land, all the Modoc were also entitled to share the claims payment money at the Klamath Reservation. In a 1901 agreement between the federal government and the Klamath tribe, payment for unallotted reservation land was put in the United States Treasury where it would earn 5 percent interest. The basic payment totaled $537,007.20. The interest on this money was paid each year to everyone on tribal rolls at the Klamath Reservation. Annual payments amounted to approximately $15 per person.

The federal government had further provided for the Klamath by setting aside 100,000 acres of forest from which timber was to be harvested and sold. The government supervised this project, and the first timber from the tract was sold in 1913. Over the years the harvesting was done in such a way that trees were always planted to replace those that were cut. In this way there was a sustained yield of timber —and lease money. Eventually selling timber became a big business, supplying $240 a year to every tribal member by 1915. By 1926 this had grown to $500 a year to each Modoc and Klamath. Thus a family of four would receive $2,000, which it could easily live on for the year. By the 1940s the timber payment money reached $800 per tribal member.

In the 1920s, 1930s, and 1940s the Modoc in both Oklahoma and Oregon achieved a degree of prosperity. The interest payments and income from the timberland and from leasing their own land enabled them to live comfor-

Peter Schonchin, the son of the Modoc leader John Schonchin, and his wife Lizzie moved to Oregon. This photograph was taken sometime before 1930.

tably. They supplemented this with farming and odd jobs. When the United States entered World War II, some Modoc enlisted in the armed forces and left the reservation to fight abroad. For the most part, the Modoc lived like their non-Indian neighbors, especially in Oklahoma where they had begun to intermarry with these neighbors.

By the 1950s, attitudes in the Bureau of Indian Affairs had changed. Whereas the Indians had in recent decades been allowed to exist peacefully together on their isolated land, the administration now favored a policy of "termination" for all Indian tribes. Reservations and tribal organizations were to be broken up. All joint economic holdings would be sold, and the resulting income distributed equally among tribal members. Thereafter the Indians would receive no special treatment from the federal government.

Public Law 587, passed on August 13, 1954, terminated the federal government's supervision of the Klamath and Modoc tribal property. The Indians were given a choice. All members of the tribes could withdraw from the tribal rolls and receive a cash settlement for their share of the tribe's property. Or they could have the United States National Bank of Oregon manage their affairs and continue to receive annual payments.

The approximately 55 Modoc in Oklahoma chose termination and cash payments. Some of the 75 to 100 Modoc in Oregon made the same choice. About four years after passage of Public Law 587, each Modoc who had chosen termination received approximately $45,000. Their land would now be taxable, as was the property of all other U.S. citizens, and they would no longer receive treatment from the Indian Health Service. The legal existence of the Modoc tribe came to an end.

Some Modoc invested their money. Others used it to educate their children. Others, unaccustomed to handling large sums, found their money was soon gone. Some slipped into poverty; their lot was especially difficult because they could no longer get any help from the Bureau of Indian Affairs.

In 1967, in an effort to regain strength as a group, the Modoc living in northeastern Oklahoma joined with several other small tribes in the area to form the Inter-Tribal Council. It was composed of three terminated tribes (the Modoc, Peoria, and Ottawa), one partially terminated tribe (the Wyandotte), and four tribes not yet terminated (the Quapaw, Miami, Eastern Shawnee, and Seneca-Cayuga). At this time the Modoc organized a new tribal government. Bert Haymon was the first chairman of the tribe, followed by Vernon "Dutch" Walker, and, in 1972, Bill Follis.

Follis's first priority as chairman was to get the Modoc reinstated as a recognized tribe so that members who needed educational and health benefits could obtain them. They finally achieved this in May of 1978, whereupon Follis became the first federally recognized chief of the Modoc Nation since Bogus Charley, who had died almost 100 years earlier. However, the constitution drafted by the Modoc tribe had not received approval of the Bureau of Indian Affairs nine years later. Nor had there been any grants for economic development that would help those Modoc living in poverty. In the late 1980s about 200 Modoc were listed on the tribal roll. Most are from Oklahoma, but some live in Oregon.

The Modoc's only tribally owned

The Modoc Tribal Office in Miami, Oklahoma, completed in 1982, serves as the headquarters and community center for the tribe. It also houses a growing archive of tribal records and photographs.

property now is a cemetery at Modoc Prairie, the old reservation, and the Tribal Office in downtown Miami, Oklahoma, that serves as a community center. At the cemetery are headstones bearing the names of such Modoc as Hooker Jim and Scarfaced Charley who had fought for their homeland and their freedom.

The Modoc are few in number today, and there is little left to represent the Modoc Nation, but at the Tribal Office, the Modoc are gathering an archive of tribal records and family letters and photographs, in the hope of preserving artifacts that explain their history. The Modoc's lives are similar to those of non-Indians in the United States, but they feel a strong pride in their heritage and history and wish to preserve these for future tribal members. They are a people who are proud that they fought for the things for which the United States has always stood: freedom, home, and a way of life. ▲

BIBLIOGRAPHY

Dillon, Richard. *Burnt-Out Fires: California's Modoc Indian War.* Englewood Cliffs, NJ: Prentice-Hall, 1973.

Hilleary, William M. *A Webfoot Volunteer,* ed. by Herbert Nelson and Preston E. Onstad. Corvallis: Oregon State University Press, 1965.

Meacham, Alfred B. *Wi-Ne-Ma (The Woman Chief) and Her People.* Hartford, CT: American Publishing Company, 1876.

Murray, Keith A. *The Modocs and Their War.* Norman: University of Oklahoma Press, 1959.

Ray, Verne. *Primitive Pragmatists: The Modoc Indians of Northern California.* Seattle: University of Washington Press, 1963.

Riddle, Jeff C. *The Indian History of the Modoc War and the Causes that Led to It.* San Francisco: Marnell Co., 1914.

Stern, Theodore. *The Klamath Tribe: A People and their Reservation.* Seattle: University of Washington Press, 1965.

THE MODOC AT A GLANCE

TRIBE *Modoc*

CULTURE AREA *Pacific Northwest*

GEOGRAPHY *Oregon/California, Northeastern Oklahoma*

LINGUISTIC FAMILY *Penutian (Lituami dialect)*

CURRENT POPULATION *200, in Oklahoma and Oregon*

FIRST CONTACT *John Charles Frémont, American, 1843*

FEDERAL STATUS *Recognized*

GLOSSARY

agent; Indian agent A person appointed by the *Bureau of Indian Affairs* to supervise U.S. government programs on a reservation and/or in a specific region.

allotment A U.S. policy, applied nationwide through the General Allotment Act of 1887, intended to bring Indians into the mainstream by breaking up tribally owned reservations and tribal government. Each tribal member was given, or allotted, a tract of land for farming.

annuities Goods, services, and cash given to a tribe each year for a specified period, based on terms of treaties or other agreements between the United States and individual tribes.

Bureau of Indian Affairs (BIA) A U.S. government agency established in 1824 and assigned to the Department of the Interior in 1849. Originally intended to manage trade and other relations with Indians and especially supervise tribes on reservations, the BIA is now involved in developing and carrying out programs to encourage Indians to manage their own affairs and to improve their educational opportunities and general social and economic well-being.

claims payments Money distributed annually to enrolled members of some Indian tribes, repaying them for the federal government's sale of unallotted, communally owned reservation land to non-Indians. Claims payments consist of the annual interest on money held in the U.S. Treasury on behalf of the various tribes to which it is due.

cultural revitalization movement A system of new rituals that develops at a time of great cultural stress and disorganization, intended to improve conditions and bring about a new and more satisfying way of life.

culture The learned behavior of human beings; nonbiological, socially taught activities; the way of life of a given group of people.

Ghost dance movement; ghost or spirit dance A religious or *cultural revitalization* movement that spread among Indians in the 1870s, centering on the belief that non-Indian newcomers would disappear and the Indians' traditional world would return if certain rituals were performed. Among the Modoc and others, these rituals included dance movements performed for days at a time.

Indian Territory An area in the south-central United States to which the U.S. government wanted to resettle Indians from other regions, especially the eastern states. In 1907 the territory became the state of Oklahoma.

Kumookumts According to Modoc myth, the creator of the world and of the tribes of humans.

la gi A Modoc village chief; a position achieved through recognition of leadership abilities.

Mo Adok Ma Klaks The name meaning "people from the South," given to the Modoc by their neighbors, the Klamath Indians. The Modoc called themselves *Ma Klaks*, "people."

reservation A tract of land set aside by treaty for occupation by and use of Indians. Some reservations were for an entire tribe; others were assigned to more than one tribe.

shaman A person who has special powers to call on various spirits to solve problems, heal the sick, or ensure success in acquiring food or in other essential activities.

sweat house An airtight hut in which rituals are held. The steam produced by pouring water over heated rocks helped a person achieve a condition of spiritual purification.

termination A U.S. policy begun under President Dwight D. Eisenhower in 1953 intended to eliminate Indians' tribal and communal organization, remove federal supervision, and end the services provided by the federal government.

treaty A contract negotiated between representatives of the United States and one or more Indian tribes. Treaties dealt with surrender of political independence, terms of payment for land, boundaries, peaceful relations, and related matters.

tribe A term used to describe a type of society consisting of a community or group of communities that occupy a common territory and are related by bonds of kinship, language, and shared traditions.

tule A tall grassy plant, or bulrush, growing in marshes, whose stems and roots were woven into baskets, mats, clothing, and other essential items.

war chief The leader of a raid or war party; a position achieved through success in previous battles. The war chief had no authority in peacetime.

INDEX

ACKNOWLEDGMENTS

Courtesy of the California State Library and Modoc Tribe of Oklahoma, pages 26, 41; Follis Collection, pages 82, 88; Landrum Collection, Shaw Historical Library, pages 43, 45, 55, 73; Library of Congress, pages 27, 28; Lowie Museum of Anthropology, The University of California at Berkeley, cover, pages 65–71, 72 (*inset*); Modoc Tribe of Oklahoma, pages 30, 33, 91; courtesy of Museum of the American Indian, Heye Foundation, pages 20, 21, 64, 72; National Archives, pages 12, 24, 29, 32, 34, 38, 50, 57, 58, 60, 74, 76, 86; Oregon Histori- cal Society, pages 15, 17, 18, 22, 23, 38, 46, 53, 56, 62, 63; Smithsonian Institution National Anthropological Archives, pages 37, 81, 89.

Maps (pages 2, 49, 78, 79) by Gary Tong.

The authors gratefully acknowledge the help of librarians and archivists at Northeastern State University and at the Oklahoma Historical Society who helped us locate materials. In addition, we thank Chief Bill Follis of the Modoc nation and tribal historian Pat Trollinger.

The editors wish to acknowledge the assistance given by Lawrence Dawson of the Lowie Museum of Anthropology (University of California at Berkeley).

ODIE B. FAULK is currently professor of history at Northeastern State University. The author of more than 40 books, Faulk is a recognized authority on Oklahoma, the American Southwest, and the Native Americans of these regions. He holds B.S., M.A., and Ph.D. degrees from Texas Tech University.

LAURA E. FAULK holds a B.S. degree from the University of Arizona and an M.A. from Northeastern State University. Long active in historical organizations, she has previously authored two volumes and for many years has reviewed books on the tribes and heritage of the American Southwest.

FRANK W. PORTER III, General Editor of INDIANS OF NORTH AMERICA, is Director of the Chelsea House Foundation for American Indian Studies. He holds an M.A. and Ph.D. from the University of Maryland, where he also earned his B.A. He has done extensive research concerning the Indians of Maryland and Delaware and is the author of numerous articles on their history, archaeology, geography, and ethnography. He was formerly Director of the Maryland Commission on Indian Affairs and American Indian Research and Resource Institute, Gettysburg, Pennsylvania, and he has received grants from the Delaware Humanities Forum, the Maryland Committee for the Humanities, the Ford Foundation, and the National Endowment for the Humanities, among others.

DATE DUE			
MAR 4 '84			

26,624

970.1   FAULK, ODIE B.
Fau

THE MODOC

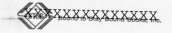